Steve Turner was born in the Midlands and worked in a variety of jobs before joining *Beat Instrumental* as a full-time writer in 1970. After two years as Features Editor, he decided to work as a freelance writer, and now contributes regularly to *Rolling Stone* and the *New Musical Express*. He also writes poetry and has had his poems published in the *Sunday Times*, *Cosmopolitan*, *Rolling Stone*, *Transatlantic Review* and several specialist poetry publications. A collection of his poetry, *Tonight We Will Fake Love*, has recently been published.

Steve Turner

CONVERSATIONS WITH ERIC CLAPTON

ABACUS edition first published in Great Britain 1976
by Sphere Books Ltd
30/32 Gray's Inn Road, London WC1X 8JL
Copyright © Steve Turner 1976

Excerpts from 'The Eric Clapton Interview', *Rolling Stone*
Copyright © 1975 by *Rolling Stone*. Reprinted by Permission.

Set in Monotype Times Roman

Printed in Great Britain by Cox & Wyman Ltd
London, Reading and Fakenham

Contents

To George and Meg, who make come-backs possible

Acknowledgments

With special thanks to those who helped me during the assembling of this book: Andrew Bailey, John and Sandy Bazlinton, Criteria Arts Ltd, Rose Clapp, Sylvia Clapton, David Andrew Davis, Ray and Jenny Hall, Jayne Harries, Pattie Harrison, Joe Marchini, Larry and Pam Norman, Alice Ormsby-Gore, Linda Osband, George and Meg Patterson, Robert Stigwood, Norman Stone, Helen Walters, Jann S. Wenner, Priscilla Wrightson. With very special thanks to Eric, without whom this book would be extremely thin.

The author and publisher would like to thank the following for supplying photographs or for giving permission for their reproduction: Mrs Clapp, 1, 2, 3, 4, 5, 6, 7, 18; Tom McGuinness, 8; A & M Records, 9; Pye Records, 10; ABC/Dunhill Records, 11; The Shelter Recording Co., 12; London Express & Feature Service, 13, 37; *The Surrey Comet*, 14; Rex Features, 15, 43; S.K.R. Photos International Ltd, 16, 20, 24, 26, 27, 32; The Decca Record Company Ltd, 17; Socion Books: from *British Beat*, Tim Phillips and Chris May, 19; Robert Stigwood Records and Tapes Ltd, 21, 22, 45; Dezo Hoffmann Ltd, 23, 25; Robert Stigwood Organisation Ltd, 28, 47, 48; Beat Publications Ltd, 29; Apple Corps Ltd, 30, 38; Tom Dowd, 31; *New Musical Express*, 33; Popsie, New York, 34; Larry Norman, 35; London Features International, 36, 42 (*Photo: Neil Jones*), 44, 46, 49, 50, 52, 53 (*Photos: Michael Putland*); Barry Plummer, 39; Dr Meg Patterson, 40 (*Photo: Larry Norman*), 41; George Terry, 51.

Introduction

I have this friend, a lady doctor, who is developing a cure for heroin addiction through an advanced form of electro-acupuncture. Her husband, a fiery Scotsman who would make a good Colonel Sanders if they should ever make the film, has in his time been a missionary, engineer, author, journalist and film maker. He knows a lot about the Bible, Asian politics, opium smuggling and mass communications involving satellites. One day they tell me that they have an addict living with them while he has treatment. There's a chance I might know him as he works in my field. Having themselves been in Hong Kong for the past decade or so the name means nothing although the track record seems impressive. His name's Eric Clapton.

My first meeting with him comes a few days later. It's the afternoon of 27 February 1974 and he's sitting on a settee dressed in a cream knitted jacket and cream slacks, hair lank and shoulder length, face clean-shaven, listening to The Doobie Brothers on a transistor radio. He seems pleased to see me – a visitor from the outside world after two weeks of being kept away because of the temptations. A visitor that knows about rock 'n' roll.

The ice isn't as difficult to crack as I had feared it might be. We get the weather done in a sentence or two, switch to the latest singles and are well into his career by the second paragraph. It's hard for me to believe. After having heard all the rumours and sensed the mystique . . . after knowing the man's sheer elusiveness as far as the journalists go . . . here I am, freelance rock writer, listening to the most amazing story of rise and fall, dope and fame, applause and frustration that I've ever heard, let alone read.

He tells me about the bitterness of Cream and how he was never happy with them and still doesn't rate their records. How he first scored dope after swearing never to tread that path because of the destruction he'd seen amongst friends. He tells me about the years spent at home in a creative twilight and the mad dashes up to London to score more dope. Also of the times the dope didn't come and he and his lady banged their heads against the walls and burned themselves with cigarettes.

Then there's Layla, his alias for George Harrison's wife Pattie whom he'd fallen in love with and been rejected by, thus creating the blues that poured out of his double album 'Layla And Other Assorted Love Songs'. 'If she was to come into this room right now,' he says at one point, 'I'd fall down at her feet.' Knowing this background, the album's strong autobiographical theme springs alive: 'Bell Bottom Blues', 'She Looked Away', 'Why Does Love Got To Be So Sad?'

As the afternoon pushes on into the evening I have to move off. My head is over-saturated with information. After having been involved in hundreds of rock interviews this seems like the first time I've actually met someone and penetrated the public image. I realise how distant rock journalists are from the real mechanics of the industry they hope to chronicle. The majority of the time the information they can give is only one step closer to the truth than record company hand-outs. The inner life of the rock business goes on untapped, unrevealed.

At this time in his life Eric has nothing more to lose except his possessions and his life and, more important, he has no product to promote. The uneasy transition from heroin addict to straight man is making him want to confess and come clean with the world after having to live the lie for so long. His system needs to be cleared. People have been nice for so long talking about his 'voluntary retirement', now it's time to let them know.

At the end of our conversation Eric makes a point of telling me that I can quote anything he's told me and use it in a story. My mind is already one step ahead at this point. Rather than that, I say, which would mean relying on my memory and also not being able to verify quotes, how about getting together over a cassette and doing the whole thing properly and then maybe selling the results to *Rolling Stone*? 'Why not,' says Eric, and two days later we do exactly that.

The first interview proper took place sprawled across the Patterson's bed – Eric at one end, me at the other. His mood was fairly despondent. He couldn't quite sort out his attitude towards the dope he'd sworn to leave and he wasn't exactly sure what there was to grasp hold of now the 'naughty powder' was gone.

'How do you feel?' I asked.

'Rough. I feel physically OK. I'm just, you know ... tension thing.'

'Is it a mental tension?'

10

'And spiritual.'

'Is it because something's unresolved? Because you don't know what's next?'

'Exactly. Exactly.'

His reasons for giving up his habit centred mainly around his lady of the past five years, whom he felt would be helped if he was strong enough to make the break with her. 'I still feel that to be a junkie is to be a part of a very elite club and that's the trouble. That's the losing part of the battle,' he explained. 'Physically it's just because it's the greatest high you'll ever have. I wouldn't have stopped in the first place if it was just for me, but the fact was that it was destroying my old lady, and I couldn't let that go on any longer. So, I still wanted to carry on myself. Now I've got even more people depending on me to come through it, you see, and I can let them down and get high again or get straight.'

Besides the emotional protection that heroin provided ('It's like surrounding yourself in pink cotton wool. Nothing bothers you whatsoever. Nothing will phase you out in any way.'), he was also convinced that it improved him as an artist initially by acting as an irritant. 'If it wasn't heroin it'd be whisky or women or something. There's got to be something,' he said, 'something that's bugging me. If I'm satisfied with everything then I've got no reason to pick up the guitar and play. It's if there's something that's annoying me or chewing at my insides, then I've got to play.'

The fact that most of his idols were junkies and 'Layla', his best album to date, was made while on heroin spurred him on in his belief. 'I always argue that all my heroes were junkies – Ray Charles, Billie Holiday, Charlie Parker . . . you name 'em. They all either die on it or they're hooked on it or they're controlled by the Mafia on it or something.

'So my argument is that it stimulates your playing – maybe not for long because sooner or later you hit the downward trail – but for a while it actually inspires you. And yet I've met people who say that I was great before I ever took the stuff. So I reckon that before I got mixed up with it I was getting high on manipulating audiences.

'I remember saying in one of my first interviews that my big ambition was to make people cry with one note, to be able to manipulate an audience like that. And that I think was giving me a high.'

His thinking that day seemed confused. He got involved with

11

heroin to screen out the emotional pain of losing Pattie. He got involved with heroin through a desire to join the musician-junkie elite. He got involved with heroin to replace the high he'd once got from performing. He stopped because of his girl-friend. He stopped because he was financially in debt. He stopped because his career had stagnated. Having not faced the questions before, he was unsure of the answers. Possibly no single factor was involved but all combined to force the changes.

It was the same unclear thinking when we discussed Cream. They broke up because of a bad review, he claimed at one point. Also given as reasons were arguments within the group and because audiences were so indiscriminate. 'I'm being told by everyone that in a month's time I'll be another man,' he said rather dejectedly, 'but right now all I can see is the suffering of today, the suffering of tomorrow and the waste of the past three years.

'If I hadn't have wasted that time I wouldn't be in the state I'm in now. I'd be so much more advanced in my career. I wouldn't be struggling to keep my name in the music papers all the time. Journalists are very kind to me – they still drop my name now and then for no reason whatsoever. I win the *Playboy* musicians' poll for four years running – but I haven't played a note!'

One of his main fears at this time was that he would never again reach the heights of brilliance that he'd reached in the past. It was almost as though he daren't pick up the guitar in case something musically inferior to the songs on 'Layla' should come out. His own pressing need to better his last work was now stifling his creativity. 'I can't play a note at the moment,' he confided. 'I can't pick up the guitar and play or do anything. I just feel it's an insult to music.'

Later that same day we picked up the story and carried on recording. During this interview Eric put the electro-acupuncture machine on his lap and fixed the clips on his ears as he was feeling slight withdrawal symptoms, a nervous twitchy edge. By the end of an hour or so he was fast asleep.

Following the weeks of treatment at Harley Street, and then completely off heroin, Eric went to a farm in North Wales. Here he was able to avoid the temptations of the city and also bring his body back into condition by working outside. He returned to London on 10 April, with his hair cropped back to Yardbirds' length and the beginnings of a beard shaded in across his face, for a 'welcome back' party thrown by manager Robert Stigwood at Soho's China

Garden restaurant. Eric arrived in a Swedish-knit pullover and ensconced himself in a corner with Pete Townshend, Elton John, George and Meg Patterson and Robert Stigwood. Later that week all the music papers came out with their 'Clapton's Back' headlines.

A few days later he flew to Miami with a few ideas for some songs he'd like to cover, a couple that he'd started to write himself, and three guys he wanted to form a band with. Within six weeks he'd recorded '461 Ocean Boulevard' and had gathered together the members of Eric Clapton and his Band. All the fears of 1 March had been overcome. Strength had been given.

On 28 May we got back together at his home in Ewhurst, Surrey, to complete the interview for *Rolling Stone*. It was my first visit to Hurtwood Edge, the house he'd bought for £30,000 in 1969 and where both Blind Faith and The Dominos had rehearsed in their formative weeks.

Because of the three years of inactivity spent watching TV, eating and sleeping, the house was in a state of disrepair during the early part of 1974. It took the arrival of Pattie Harrison later that year to get it looking more like home again. 'It's all accidental,' says Eric of Hurtwood. 'There's so much rubble . . . different things that are there for no purpose whatsoever, that I feel comfortable in it. I like the accidental untidiness of it all. I can just flop down anywhere or pick up something that's just rubble.

'The thing I like about other musicians' homes is that they can get it together to install pin tables, pool tables and things like that in pretty quick time and yet I still haven't got round to that. The nearest thing I've got is a darts board which is up in the attic.'

Activity at Hurtwood fluctuates between the large room pictured on the Blind Faith album sleeve where all the music equipment and albums live and a smaller room nearby where the TV and video are installed. Most of the albums are black, whether they be reggae, blues, gospel or soul. There are hardly any white rock albums. One night when carrying my bags up to a bedroom Eric commented on the weight. I explained that this was because I'd brought down copies of all his albums to bring questions to mind during the interviews. 'Really?' he said, 'Can I see them?' I pulled them out and he took away 'Eric Clapton', 'Disraeli Gears', 'Wheels Of Fire', and 'On Tour With Delaney And Bonnie' to play to Pattie that night as he wanted her to hear them and hadn't got copies himself.

Favourite video-viewing material is 'Monty Python's Flying Circus' – 'Mr Neutron' being a particular favourite. 'I've always loved loonies,' says Eric. 'I like loonies. I identify with them. The Python type of humour is the kind that breeds in rock 'n' roll bands of its own accord. Every band has got its own banter which is pretty cliquey to someone on the outside. It's pretty hard to understand sometimes. You develop this sort of rapport which they've got amongst themselves and it's very much the same sort of thing.'

A year or so later while on Paradise Island, Eric was to be furious when the American 'TV World' Viewing Guide panned the first Python series which was being screened across the US referring to it as 'over-graduate humour'. It took a glowing review the same week by *Time* to restrain his anger.

During a break in that day's interviewing Eric played me the tapes of '461 Ocean Boulevard'. I was surprised as Eric must have expected me to be. After the grit and gristle of 'Layla' here was something so tender and relaxed ... and where was that sweet aching guitar? It's my policy never to comment on first hearing and so I kept my reaction to head noddings and the occasional escape of breath. Later, having overcome the effects of having my pre-conceptions jarred, I really came to love '461', and 'Give Me Strength' became the song that summed up Eric's come-back period.

Asked about the possibility of touring again during our first interview Eric had replied, 'Well, it's a battle for me because, you see, the music scene is so entrenched with drugs that I've either got to go straight back on or reach the point where I can say "No thanks". That's what touring means to me right now, not the actual bread that I could make or the audiences that I could please but the problem that I will have when someone walks in the dressing room with something ... which always does happen.'

By the time the album had been recorded he was practically hostile towards dope. The tension had been resolved and no longer did he believe, as he had done two months before, that heroin actually improved the quality of a singer's voice.

After rehearsals in Barbados the new band took to the road kicking off in Scandinavia and continuing in the US. In July *Rolling Stone* printed 'The Eric Clapton Interview' as their front-page story. Simultaneously a two column write-up on the cure and comeback was printed in *Time*. This was the first time he'd spoken to the press in five years and he hasn't been interviewed since.

As the only authoritative source of information on Eric's addiction, the *Rolling Stone* interview shot a few ripples through the world's press – the hottest aspects being his admitted involvement with heroin and his relationship with Pattie Harrison, whom he'd referred to in the interview as 'the wife of my best friend', going on to say that the best friend was into Transcendental Meditation.

Of the many letters sent to me in response to the interview most seemed happy that their hero had talked at last and happier still that he'd kicked his habit. For some though it'd destroyed their preconceptions which had up until then been embalmed in a solution of mystique. 'The Eric Clapton I know,' wrote someone from North Carolina, 'has so much simplicity with so much understanding. So mild and yet so resolute. A mind so placid and a life so active. Why did not Turner examine this?'

One letter complained about Eric's lack of fondness for Cream. 'I am very depressed after reading "The Eric Clapton Interview". Despite what anyone says, Cream were a wonderful experience to us white suburban punks. It made a lot of money for some people but more important it gave us a different sound and heroes who were cool without killing anyone. How many of us had heard a drum solo before "Toad"? Clapton, Bruce and Baker inspired us to become musicians and to appreciate instrumentation. Eric Clapton was "God" once, but I think the seventies Clapton is a cunt. Is Ginger Baker our last sixties folk hero?'

A couple of correspondents complained about Eric's drunkenness on stage during the tour that was in progress when the interview came out, contrasting his behaviour with the opinions he'd given. 'After I read "The Eric Clapton Interview" I couldn't stop laughing,' wrote a fan from Dunkirk, New York. 'What he said about trying to please a crowd at a concert was an awful lie. Eric Clapton stunk when he came to Buffalo. First he walked out on stage so drunk he couldn't sing worth shit. He was constantly cursing the crowd. Many of the fans left before the show was over only to miss members of The Band lift Clapton up and carry his drunken corpse off-stage.'

Eric's own feelings about the interview came out when we were together in the Bahamas in 1975. I asked him whether there'd been any comeback as far as he was concerned. 'Only the dope thing. Because we did that revealing side to the interview it tends to prejudice people towards me. They look at me as though I'm a bit of a freak.

'Also, when we set up the tour of Australia someone took up the thing with the Immigration Office that I was actually an undesirable alien. We almost didn't get in there because of the fact that I'd coughed up about all that. I wish in a way that I hadn't done it. I wish I'd kept it to myself. I know I was dying to tell someone but now it comes back to me in strange ways. People like to ask me about it all the time.' Did he regret doing it then? 'It's not a question of regret. It's just that it was the only thing I could've said at the time.'

The idea for extending the *Rolling Stone* interview into a book didn't come about until December 1974. I called Eric up over Christmas and put the idea to him. He liked it and agreed to discuss it further with Robert Stigwood when they met up in Rio during January. When this was cleared our next interview was arranged and on 19 March I went down to Hurtwood for two days.

This time around he was not so comfortable talking about himself, preferring for us to just drink together, watch endless hours of TV or play records. The first night we got nothing down on tape and he promised to be up by ten in the morning so that we could get to work. At one-thirty the following afternoon Eric appeared downstairs in a kimono 'borrowed' from a Japanese hotel, just about ready for breakfast. At three o'clock we were ready to record and managed to get two or three hours done. However, he later changed his mind about completing the whole project in the two days set aside, as he felt tired of talking about himself. He said he would prefer it if we could continue next week. I was to get well used to these delays before the book was completed.

For the next session he came to my London flat dressed in a blue turtle-neck pullover and a check lumberjack's coat. We started off by eating fish and chips in a nearby café discussing the 'Tommy' film which I had seen a preview of but which he wasn't to see until the premiere. I hadn't been too enchanted with it on first viewing, feeling that Ken Russell had over-indulged his imagination from start to finish instead of giving light and shade. However, Eric was knocked out by it when he went along later that same week after apparently almost wanting to give it a miss after my thumbs down.

Back at the flat he seemed freer in his conversation than he had been at his home environment or at any time when Pattie was around. He left at six o'clock to go to Stigwood's office and agreed to complete the interview before setting off for an Australian tour.

On 29 March Robert Stigwood threw a thirtieth birthday party for Eric at his Tudor mansion in Stanmore on the outskirts of London. It was the stars night out – Rod and Britt, Elton, Ringo,

Twiggy, Ron Wood. Eric's former lady Alice was there, and his mum spent the evening wandering around utterly thrilled with the occasion saying, 'Hello, I'm Eric's mum. Who are you?' Apparently she stayed up 'til five in the morning singing pub songs while Elton banged away on the piano.

Our next interview got cancelled and last-minute attempts were made to get me out to him on tour in Australia because he was only likely to be back in England for a week before going out to the Bahamas for a year. When the Australian attempt failed there was only one week left in which to finish everything off, but it was when he returned that the crash occurred.

'I was trying to get past this juggernaut because there was hardly any room and it was either that or slamming on the brakes and risking a skid, so I just tried to drive through,' he recalled later. 'I don't know what he did, but he hit me on the door and I just stood on the brakes and stopped the fucking car. The car was still there . . . it was where I stopped it but the lorry bounced off the car and was in the bushes across the road. Me and the car actually moved him over the road.

'It was too quick to know what had happened to me or how close to death I'd come. It was too quick to consider. I was actually taken out of the car smiling. When the firemen came to cut me out I was sitting there with blood pouring down my face smiling. So I must have been grateful to be alive even though I didn't know.'

For a few days afterwards, after an initial night in hospital, he was sleeping for most of the day and his hearing had not returned in one ear. Some American radio stations were already treating the accident with all the importance surrounding a major rock fatality – maybe fearing that his ear injury would be permanent and shatter his career. Because of the trouble, our appointment was made for his last Friday in England before flying to the Bahamas on the Sunday. On the Thursday I recieved a telegram, 'Can't make it tomorrow. Lots of appointments. Love Eric.'

It seemed that the project was doomed. Half a book would never do. The only possible alternative now was to catch him in the Bahamas while he rested there for three weeks prior to rehearsals and his first US tour of the year. On 13 May I left London for Nassau via Miami.

Paradise Island lies about one quarter of a mile to the north of Nassau and can be reached by a long span bridge. The house that Eric and Pattie chose to rent for the rest of 1975 lay to the west of the island, the plot of land stretching from a private beach on the northern edge down to a private jetty on the south where their own motorboat could take them across the water into downtown Nassau.

Mostly the island is for holiday makers and it's major activities take place within the environs of the individual hotels – private bathing, dancing, eating, cabaret and shopping. Attached to the Brittanica Hotel is a well equipped Casino and nearby lies a golf course. Many tourists hire out small Honda motorcycles for $10 a day and travel around the island and up over the bridge into Nassau.

The house that Eric rented was built around ten years ago for 1\frac{1}{2}$ million by an American lawyer called Sam Clapp. It has the best of everything: roofing imported from Spain; glass imported from America; antiques imported from Britain; commissioned paintings. Everything built to order. It's Spanish in style – white-walled, mosaic-floored portico, the face lit up at night. Somehow though it's not home. It lacks soul. Pattie says it's more a party house than a home.

The beach that runs directly outside the house is the beach that The Beatles ran along in 'Help'. It gave me a strange feeling to be with Pattie on the beach, to think about that, and then remember fifteen-year-old me watching The Beatles in that movie and wishing I was them. Later in the week as I cycled under the trees into Nassau I remembered all those sequences with the four lads cycling the same streets in search of the lost ring.

Eric's reasons for spending a year in the Bahamas are twofold. Firstly it allows him a tax-free year as he won't be a British resident and secondly it allows him to be close enough to America, and Miami in particular, without actually being there. It's a good work base. Also it's a place for his best friends to come on holiday.

During the week I was there Albhy Galuten, a session musician from Criteria Studios in Miami who had played on all of Eric's last three studio albums, was hanging out. George Terry, guitarist with Eric's band, came over with his lady. Carl Richardson, an engineer from Criteria, dropped by and Stephen Stills was threatening to arrive any minute in his hundred-foot boat which was presently docked in Miami. Carl Radle was also expected to visit, and when it was learned that flights in from Miami were heavily booked Eric was casually asking around how much it would cost them to charter a flight from Miami to Nassau just to get him over.

The lifestyle in the Bahamas is fairly relaxed for Eric. A typical day means getting up at eleven, breakfasting, playing records, drinking and playing backgammon with Albhy, Pattie or Simon, a young English boy who looks after the house.

By four or five o'clock he's likely to want to crash out for three or four hours and then spring back into action with more music, drink and backgammon, with maybe a meal and a floodlit game of badminton to finish off the day. Because of the undisciplined life and the lunatic edge which was being nurtured courtesy of the fridge full of drink, such seriousness as interviews became an unwanted confrontation with the real world.

Eric seemed to want things to 'just happen' spontaneously, but with my time limited to five days gambles like that weren't in order. He somehow wanted to delay the confrontation as it seemed so far removed from the banter that had worked up in the house. At times I became frustrated with his lack of concern and Albhy or Pattie would have to explain to me that Eric found the interviews too serious and just wanted me to loon around and pick up my information in the process.

In the end two fairly lengthy interviews did take place, both of them just after he'd got up in the morning and before the drinks had started. The results were good and I was relieved to have completed my work with the world's most uninterviewable man. I could see by then exactly why he avoided the press. It's not for reasons of mystique preservation or because he has doubts about them, but because he has doubts about himself and the value of his opinions. He genuinely does believe he has nothing to say.

In spite of all the fame and acclaim there's still an insecurity about him. A lot of this comes through in the interviews – his constant playing down of his own talent, his fears that his peak is over, the break-away comment when he feels he's being too serious. One *Rolling Stone* reader wrote to me, 'In spite of being impressed by Clapton's ostensibly genuine humility I could not help but be disturbed by his continual undermining and/or underrating of his own talents. Humility is one thing, a desirable trait that levels everyone off, especially artists, but self-depreciation is something that can only lead to a suicide, whether of the total self, or of one's talents.'

Much of this could stem back to his childhood when he discovered at the age of twelve that the people he'd always known as his parents were his grandparents. He'd been born illegitimately to their daughter, and was never to know his real father. There have been many who, after feeling an element of rejection or social disgrace, have used rock 'n' roll both as a refuge for their alienation

19

and as a means of gaining the acceptance and adoration they feel cheated of. It's only later that they realise the acceptance is only for the image they project or the pleasure they bring, not for them as people.

'I feel that this kind of discovery either makes or breaks a person,' says a close friend, 'and I think it made Eric, musically. He says he was never into music until that time and it made him, but all the pain and hurt of it still remain with him. He tries not to face up to reality, he fights shy of it. His silliness is his way of fighting people off from looking inside him. He doesn't like to be looked inside.'

Hopefully though, the following interviews will give as close a look as one is likely to get – in the words of Eric Clapton himself. The original *Rolling Stone* question and answer format has been kept so that his comments can be seen in the context they were given in and so that his thinking can be observed at work. Sometimes, as in the 'Presence of the Lord' section, our interview turned into a discussion/argument and this has been retained in its original form.

London, 1975

At This Point in Time

28 May 1974,
Ewhurst, Surrey

Why the three-year layoff?

I'd over-exposed myself. I'd worked so hard and played in front of so many people that it frightened me into hiding for a bit. And I think it's probably going to happen again. I'll go out and work and play for three years and then for the next three years I'll go and hibernate somewhere else! You can't keep at it all the time, I'm sure of that.

So how've you been spending your time?

Hibernating! I played a lot. I played here at home probably more than I do now but without really getting anything done. Just keeping my hand in.

Were you writing at all?

Sometimes, but most of the stuff I did in that period was so gloomy that I wouldn't use it now. Also, when you sit and play on your own you write on an acoustic guitar, and so if you try and place it in the context of a band it doesn't mean a thing. You have to change it around to suit the sound of the group.

Was there any outside pressure put on you to play again?

No, none whatsoever. I mean, I was the one who put pressure on myself in the end. It just got to the point where in order to live in the manner I was living in, I was going to have to start selling cars and guitars and stuff like that because I was running out of money very fast. And I just thought, well, if I'm going to have to start doing that then it's all wrong, because the minute you start you'll sell everything in a week and then you'll go out and start stealing things.

So you really reached a crisis point?
Yeh.

Because another part of your problem was that the 'naughty powder' was eating up your money as well, wasn't it?

Yeh. I mean, it's expensive. It's very expensive to live like that.

So it was destroying you both creatively and financially . . . really pushing you onto the ledge?

Yeh, and it takes away your freedom because you can't go anywhere without having to set up another rendezvous. It's not the way to live.

Did you end up hating it?

The naughty powder itself? I don't think it's that. It's not what you take, it's what makes you take it – and I hated that. If I see other people now in that condition I really get the horrors. I mean, it makes you look so ugly. It really does.

To get down to specifics – it's because you've now come off the stuff that you've been able to get it together, go back on the road and record – right?

I couldn't have done it with . . . I couldn't have done both. And I know it was probably something I *had* to go through. If I had the opportunity to change it all again I'd probably leave it as it is because perhaps it took that to get me back on my feet again. You can't go up without coming down.

Is it still a struggle?

Yeh. It's not a struggle to avoid getting hooked on anything again – it's just a struggle to please all the people that you want to please. That's always a struggle. I think it's fatal, though, to announce that you've reformed and that you're never going to go back again. The thing about being a musician is that it's a hard life and I know that the minute I get on the road I'm going to be doing all kinds of crazy stuff. It's just that kind of life.

How did it feel when you knew people were saying 'Eric Clapton's a junkie'?

It bothered me in a way because at the time I didn't want to be found out. I wanted to keep it a secret. But the thing is, the minute you try to keep a secret, everyone knows it already! But if I come across someone these days who looks like they're on it, I get pissed off and I don't want to talk to them unless they'll listen. And I know they won't – because I didn't!

Is it difficult for you to come out like this and declare your problem?

Yeh, because I still don't believe it was the powder. It was just a weakness on my part to face myself.

What did you think of people on H before you got involved?

I used to think they were cunts. Why waste your time? Why waste your life? And then I had my first taste and thought, 'Oh, you know, one snort can't do me any harm.' But ... dead wrong! Wrong again! After the first time I suddenly understood why junkies were junkies. Delaney and Bonnie once took me to see a well-known musician and he couldn't get up out of his chair he was so wasted. I just felt sorry for him. I thought he was a bit of a dick for letting himself get into that state but I felt sorry for him, and this was before I'd ever been near the stuff. When I took my first taste and got my first high then I understood everything immediately – why they do it, why they smash drug stores to get it, why they mug people to score. . . .

So why haven't there been any interviews?

I was frightened – really! I felt I had nothing to say and if you've got nothing to say then it's better not to say anything at all. I find it hard doing interviews even now because I still don't think I've got that much to say about the music. I mean, I'll talk about anything you like, but for some reason I find it very difficult to talk about music. I can talk about the reasons for it and the methods of doing it. Also, when you're on H the last thing you want is to be bothered by people. A telephone ringing or a doorbell can drive you up the wall.

Have you been at all conscious of building up a mystique?

Only when people tell me I have. I mean, I got that from Robert, (Stigwood), my manager. He said that because I hadn't played for three years and hadn't really appeared except for the Bangla and Rainbow gigs, that I was therefore much more saleable and my market had gone up and such like. But, you know, I'll believe it when I see it. Perhaps it's true.

How long did it take to get '461 Ocean Boulevard' together?

I went up to Wales and stayed there for a while and did some farming. Then I came back here and within a week I was off to the States to record. It was just a question of saying, 'Look, Robert, I want to work.' And he says, 'OK, you're going to work now . . . hard!' I like that kind of option because it doesn't give me time to sit around and think about it and have doubts. I just have to do it. I arrived in Miami without anything besides a couple of acoustic things I wanted to do. As far as making an electric album, I had no idea! So we just built it there and then.

You literally wrote it in the studio?

Yeh. It was time-consuming for the other musicians and for the engineers and all that, but they got into the swing of it in the end and everyone was sharing the load.

What musicians were you using?

I used Carl (Radle) and a couple of mates of his from Tulsa – Jamie (Oldaker) plays drums and Dr Dick Simms is on organ, and they're the sort of nucleus of the band. Then we've got Yvonne Elliman who'd be playing either acoustic or electric guitar and singing, and George Terry, a guy I met in Miami, who plays guitar, writes and does good vocal harmonies. Sort of a six-piece. I've no idea how we're going to arrange it for stage yet. It'll have to be sorted out at rehearsals.

When did you decide on the line-up?

It was just a question of first come, first served. People who wanted to play on the album did start showing up as well as some who just wanted to play. Like Steve Stills showed up and was just a bit too late because we'd already settled into our groove and anyone else added would have been a diversion. We did about three weeks' recording, and the first two weeks whoever happened to be in the studio at the time was on the sessions, you know. After that we got into a groove and stayed there.

How much material did you record?

About thirty tracks. We just went in and did as many as we could. We could have booked the studios for twenty-four hours a day but the routine was days of sunshine and evenings of recording.

How many songs did you attempt to record at each session?

We'd try and get three out but would be happy with two. What we'd do is we'd walk in and jam and then we'd listen to it back and write the song. You know, pick out a riff, or part of the jam that was good, and then write a song with it. We really got it going in the end. A lot of the stuff that we did like that didn't get used, though. Probably seventy-five per cent of what we recorded was other people's songs which I'd always wanted to do. You know, I always put one Robert Johnson song on my albums because he was my guru, or is my guru, or something. A lot of the best stuff didn't go on the album because we just thought it was too laid back.

How did you go about choosing the material which wasn't self written?

Well, they're just things that I've known for a long time. Songs that I've always liked and that creep back into my memory. I just wanted to get them off my chest.

You see, I let Tom Dowd produce the album and the groove we got into was getting so laid back, so quiet and delicate, that I just thought – no, they won't want to hear it. Because there were lots of mistakes in it, and yet the feel was so good. But then Tom thought it would be better to combine, you know, have some of that and also some of the heavier stuff. And he's right, in a way.

Do you have some conception of what people want to hear from you then?

Yeh ... and I know they're not going to get it! I know they want me to go on and, you know, try and blow everyone off-stage with lead guitar but they're not going to get that. I mean, they'll get a bit of that because I'm that way inclined. I do like to have a bit of a blow now and then. But it's not fair on the band that way and I really like to maintain a sort of sharing of the responsibility with the group, you know. I found that with The Dominos we just got into a thing where they once again became a back-up band.

Do you think the fastest-guitar-in-the-west syndrome has now burned itself out?

As far as I'm concerned, it has. It doesn't seem to as far as the market is concerned though. The market still wants more and more of that but it really bores me to tears to hear people play that way. My driving philosophy about making music is that you can reduce it all down to one note if that note is played with the right kind of feeling and with the right kind of sincerity. I'd love to knock an audience cold with one note but what do you do for the rest of the evening (laughs)?

Is it still your ambition, as you once said it was, to make an audience cry with a single note?

Yeh, I think so. You see, it happens to me all the time. I put a record on the record player and just to hear Stevie Wonder sing 'Bridge Over Troubled Water' or something like that would, if I'm alone, make me cry. Literally just weep. But you see you've got to be an afficianado in the first place for that to happen, so it's very difficult. Like I've said before, it's an ability which only very few musicians have of producing one note in a certain context in the middle of a solo – just one note or one lick that can make an audience en masse quiver with emotion.

You told me before that you need an irritant in order to create. Have you still got that?

The irritant now is just getting the band together, you know, and being the leader of the band. That's pretty irritating, I can tell you! Because the minute they know you're the leader you get all their complaints and hassles. That's my blues at the moment.

How're you going out this time around?

Just Eric Clapton and his Band.

Are you looking forward to returning to the road?

Oh yeh. I've been sitting around here for a week now and I'm getting really edgy, bored. Because for those three weeks in Miami it just cooked so fast and so strong we should have perhaps gone straight to a gig from there instead of taking a pause. But I'm sure we'll pick up the threads.

Were you surprised to get things going so quickly in Miami?

Yeh, yeh. I was very worried when I got there. I had the panics. It took me a couple of days just to learn to create from nothing – to groove on whatever was happening, and then it was alright. But I always get that when I sit down and think about something. I've got it now about the tour to a certain extent. Whether or not we can get all the people to come and see us, that kind of thing, which is so silly really. It's only when you sit down and worry about it that you ever think about it at all.

26

You say you always needed pain to create and yet you enjoyed heroin because it took away the pain. How do you explain that one?

It's a paradox, in a way, because in order to create you've got to have pain and the thing about that stuff is that it takes away the pain which you probably want. I mean, I enjoy the pain in a way because I know I can make use of it if I don't tamper with it. You can take away the pain by playing the guitar, just making music and seeing people enjoying themselves on it. But when you start using chemicals and naughty powder, then I mean what do you do with that? I mean, you just get trapped in a hole which you're lucky to get out of really. The thing that knocked me out most of all about getting off was the fact that I could feel again, you know. I don't care where I'm going, up or down, or whatever they do to me, as long as they let me keep my feelings.

Did you feel they'd been excluded?

Yeh, well, I'd done that to myself, you see. Because at the time we were doing 'Layla', my feelings were so intense that I just couldn't handle them. So that's why I started to cancel them out and that in turn becomes the pain. People used to come around here and try and take me off by the scruff of the neck and say come on, get out, come with me. I mean, people even considered kidnapping me and taking me somewhere where I'd have to get myself together. And like that's the pain, the fact that afterwards you realise all the people you hurt by doing that.

So it was the crisis that happened around 'Layla' time that sent you into it?

Yeh. There were quite a lot of factors involved. Also, I mean, I used to go on about how I wanted to have a voice like Ray Charles and everyone had said that he was one of those, that he had that problem, and that's why he sang like that. Now I know that that is utter bullshit. I've got the first album that he made and his voice there was unbelievable, you know, and it's just got nothing to do with what you take or what you put in your bloodstream.

Whose music turns you on now?

Whenever I put my new album on and start to think it sounds great, I always put Stevie Wonder on afterwards just to get pulled down again! He's the one for me. I think he's got it well covered.

27

I think when it comes down to it, I always go for singers. I don't buy an album because I like the lead guitar. I always like the human voice most of all.

Again, why do you think people will be surprised at the new album?

Because I'm still being thought of as the lead guitarist and that's not me, it really isn't. I'm just an unskilled-labourer musician who finds it difficult to get in tune, let alone play lead guitar solos. What I tried to achieve on that album was satisfying the people I was playing with. That's what I really like doing – just sitting down with people who play anything and finding the lowest common denominator that we can all groove with and getting something going. It's not 'Who's going to take the front now?' I mean, *you* take the front now, *I'll* take the front now! It's everyone together, all at the same time.

So what's your function in the new band?

The leader of the band. Occasionally I'll hit a lick that'll blow someone's mind, I know that. And if it's not mine, it'll be someone elses, only they can't have it all the time. That's probably what people want – just one long lead guitar solo.

Why did you choose Yvonne Elliman? For her role in 'Jesus Christ Superstar'?

Because she was there. I didn't choose her, I just let her sing on the album because I wanted to hear a female voice. I hadn't sung with a girl before, actually, and it was quite a turn-on.

You believe in chance quite a bit then?

Yeh. That's my faith. Uncertainty, not knowing what's coming next. That's really my faith. I don't want to know – I just want it to be now and happening. It's very hard to be that way because I've already pre-arranged the fact that, OK, they were the people that were on the album and now I've arranged for them all to be in Barbados for the rehearsals. Whereas if I'm actually living on the edge properly, I just say, 'OK. See you around sometime,' and turn up in Barbados and probably play with the housemaid and whoever. Really that's what it should be. But it's hard to live like that.

To your mind, is the album related to blues?

Well, it's a funny kind of album in that way. It's got several different

28

kinds of things on it because I'm always worrying about who I'm going to please apart from pleasing myself. So there's probably, like, a couple of blues things on there and a couple of slightly folky things and a bit of rock as well.

Does the fact that you're playing less intense music mark a change in attitude?

It's not a change in attitude so much as a . . . change in attitude (laughs)! It's loitering with intense! (laughs). No, really, I'd like it to be that way, but I know that when I get up on stage I'm going to be very tempted to play loud and get nasty and do lots of naughty things with my guitar, but I'm fighting it with everything I've got. It does you in, all that, it really does. I'll tell you about something. Once with The Dominos we dropped some acid in San Francisco, of all places to drop acid, and apart from the fact that the guitar was made of rubber, every bad lick I had – every naughty lick, blues lick, whatever you want to call it – turned the audience into all these devils in sort of red coats and things. And then I'd play a sweet one and they all turned into angels. I prefer playing to angels, personally.

A good enough reason!

(Laughs.) It is, when you think about it. It is. I mean, I just hate to think what all that heavy music is doing to all these poor people in terms of . . . like, eating raw meat. It's the same kind of thing, do you know what I mean? The seeds that you sow are the ones that you reap. If you're going to make everyone feel naughty, then they'll be naughty and we can't have that.

What about the George Harrison tour rumours which sounded good to your ears when you first heard them?

They still do sound good except that he's got a lot on his plate at the moment, let alone thinking about touring. Sure, I'd love to work with him on-stage. I really would. But he's got his own fish to fry and so've I.

What's the best Eric Clapton rumour that you've heard?

(Laughs.) That there are strong chances that I'll be committed very soon! Actually, I've heard some funny rumours about me, you know, about what I'm supposed to be doing, where I am, what I have been doing . . . and none of them were anywhere near it, really.

Perhaps that's what comes of not giving interviews!

No, it doesn't, really. They'll still . . . 'cos I'll still hedge even with my mates, let alone what I say to the press. I mean, it's rumours. I even tell rumours about myself. It's all speculation.

You've been acting in Ken Russell's film of 'Tommy'?

Oh, yeh. Phew, that was quite a number, I can tell you! Acting out a part! They had this church hall . . . I mean, it wasn't mucking about. They had me there to play the preacher and I had to be the preacher 'cos they had about sixty or seventy people who really were in a bad way. Well, I mean, they say they're in a bad way. They couldn't keep their arms under control, couldn't see and all that, and it was quite heavy having to be their preacher for the day.

What role was that?

The preacher. Tommy's looking for a cure and I'm just one of the geezers he goes to and it doesn't work again. He still can't see and hear. The thing about it is that it's about this chick who can heal you if you kiss her feet. I mean, she's not there – it's a statue of her, and the chick is Marilyn Monroe. So they've got this big statue of Marilyn Monroe and they're leading all these blind people and paraplegics and kissing her feet and I'm the loony in charge (laughs).

Do you have to play guitar?

Yeh. Well, I had it around my neck. I have to sing 'Eyesight For The Blind' – Richie Havens did it on the 'Tommy' album.

Do you ever think beyond the end of this tour?

I can't even face tomorrow. It's going to be another three years before they wear me out. And apparently, because of my tax problems, I've got to do one of those Stones' numbers – you know, I've got to leave the country for a year at some point because they've got me by the short and curlies, I can tell you. So, I'm on the move, I'm on the road. It don't matter. They'll never get me. They can take my body but they can't have anything else (laughs)!

Good Old Days, 1945–63

How was it that you came to play guitar in the first place?

It was a very indirect process. I had one bought for me, gave up very quickly, and then I sort of picked it up a few years later when I had nothing else to turn to. I literally had to make money with it in order to buy a drink and have a sandwich in the pub. I think that's a pretty good incentive, actually. It's when you start making so much money that you don't need to go out to work and play to live that it becomes bad. That was another of the reasons for me laying off. I just knew that there was no necessity for me to go and play in front of an audience, except to please them. That's not right because then you start worrying about whether you're going to please them or not.

Did the money you earned in turn deprive you of having the blues then?

Yeh. You can't play the blues on a full stomach, can you? My attitude to money is that I don't carry it on me and if it's given to me I throw it away on the first nonsense I can buy, because if you get more than you need it burns a hole in your pocket.

You've been quoted as saying that you can't play guitar.

I still can't, you know. If I was to pick up a guitar now I'd have to relearn everything I'd ever played. Of course I can remember the chord structures but what I'm talking about is creative guitar playing – picking up the guitar and playing something I've never played before.

Were you at all surprised to find yourself rated top guitarist in various musical polls?

Yeh, I was, really, because I didn't think I was. I think I'm probably the fiftieth if anything.

So who would you shuffle about in the top five?

That's a very difficult question. B. B. King, Joe Walsh, Pete Townshend, George Harrison – his slide playing. Do you mean

31

musicians that are still living, because there's Duane Allman, Jimi Hendrix. . . .

Did you really relate to Hendrix?

Oh, I loved him. There will never be another Jimi Hendrix. He was the best. When he died I went out in the garden and cried all day because he'd left me behind. Not because he'd gone, but because he hadn't taken me with him. It just made me so fucking angry. I wasn't sad, I was just pissed off.

What gives you most confidence in your playing? Is it approval by people you dig as opposed to awards, acclaims, record sales and good reviews?

Yeh. It's a combination. If I didn't get the *Playboy* Award this year or next year or whatever that would affect me. I'd think about it and wonder why. Probably not very much, though, because I've always thought of it in terms of being like a bit of a con merchant, really. I know in my own self that I'm not really deserving of that because I know better players. I know millions of better players. Like George Terry, for instance. I've been thinking all this time, oh, I'm getting away with it again this year.

What's your domestic background?

I was semi-adopted. I was brought up by my grandparents because my mother went away when I was very young and got married to someone. So I've got a stepfather, but I don't see them because they've got a family themselves and they live in Canada. From there I just grew up in all the local schools around Ripley in Surrey and went to art school.

What sort of kid were you at school?

I was the one that used to get stones thrown at me because I was so thin and couldn't do Physical Training very well (laughs)! One of those types. I was always the seven-stone weakling. I used to hang out with three or four other kids who were all in that same kind of predicament. The outcasts. They used to call us 'the loonies' (laughs).

What effect did that have on you?

It was quite nice in a way because we started up a little clique.

1 *Top:* Eric at eight months *(right)* with cousin Barry, Ripley Green, Surrey 2 *Above:* Eric at three, with his father 3 *Right:* Eric at eight, with a 'friend', Ripley Green, Surrey—'I definitely had a lovely time growing up'

4 *Top left:* Eric at twelve 5 *Top right:* Eric at fourteen, with his Mum, outside Holly Field School, Surbiton—'I was always a seven-stone weakling' 6 Eric aged sixteen pictured with friends near Richmond Bridge, Surrey, 1961

7 *Top:* Christmas 1964, Woking, Surrey 8 *Above:* The Roosters playing the Jazz Cellar, Kingston, 1963 *left to right:* Eric, Robin Mason, Terry Brennan, Tom McGuinness and Ben Palmer

9 *Top:* Sonny Terry and Brownie McGhee 'mysteriously got played on "Family Favourites"... It hit something inside' 10 *Above:* Sonny Boy Williamson—'Quite frightening really'

11 *Above:* B. B. King, an early influence

12 *Above:* Freddie King—'A funkier style of playing'

13 *Top:* The Yardbirds with their manager Giorgio Gomelski *(extreme left)* and Eric *(second from right)* 14 *Above:* The Yardbirds playing at The Toby Jug, Tolworth, 20 January 1964 *left to right:* Chris Dreja, Paul Samwell-Smith, Jim McCarty, Keith Relf and Eric.

15 *Left:* Eric as a Yardbird

16 *Left:* After leaving The Yardbirds, March 1965

17 *Top:* John Mayall and The Bluesbreakers during an album cover session—'I was sleepy-eyed and didn't know what to do so I went and bought a *Beano' left to right:* John Mayall, Eric, John McVie and Hughie Flint 18 *Above:* The last performance with John Mayall, June 1966, Stoke Hotel, Guildford—'I was always looking for somewhere else'

Although we were underprivileged, we were the first ones to get Buddy Holly records and things like that. I mean, we were considered freaks.

What happened at art school?
I played records in the lunch break most of the time! That's also where I started to play guitar and began listening to blues records all the time.

Who in particular?
Muddy Waters, Big Bill Broonzy ... I could go on for hours. There's no point. Just the blues.

How did you get to hear these records in the first place?
I think they used to play a couple of them on the radio. It's unbelievable that things like that were getting through, but they were. Chuck Berry was getting played and I definitely heard Big Bill Broonzy records on the radio. And Sonny Terry and Brownie McGhee. I used to get catches of these things which sounded much better than Jimmy Young, Max Bygraves and Frankie Vaughan to me. So I started looking around and buying them. I still started out by liking Holly and Berry and people like that who were the first things I ever bought, but then I'd read things on the back of album covers like 'rock 'n' roll has its roots in blues' and stuff like that. And so I thought what's that all about? I'll have to find out.

How were you performing at this point?
Casually. I wasn't professional, didn't have a band. I was just a blues afficianado with a guitar, attempting to sing. When Mick (Jagger) got a sore throat, I used to get up and dep. for him at the Ealing club.

Were the old days, good old days?
Of course. Yeh, lovely times. Probably because it was another clique thing. We felt honoured to be members of this sort of club of people who just liked rhythm and blues records. It was like security in a way, and it was nice.

Do you ever yearn to be back there again?
Yeh, of course I do. I feel much more alone these days. Whatever

I've got to achieve, I've got to achieve on my own. In the old days it seemed that there was always a crowd you hung out with.

Why were you eventually kicked out of art school?

Because there was a test at the end of the year where you had to walk in with your folder and show them how much work you'd done, and I was the one with the least amount of work done.

So it was just on that basis?

Yeh, just about. And, also because I was a general nuisance. Like I told you, I was playing records most of the time and making a fool of myself and getting drunk in the pub in the lunch hour. I was a generally undesirable influence!

What happened after that?

I bummed around for a bit. I tried busking around Kingston and Richmond and, of course, it was the beat scene then, so if you sat in a pub and played 'San Francisco Bay Blues' and stuff like that you'd get a drink and a sandwich and perhaps even somewhere to sleep for the night. Then my mum and dad, that's to say my grandparents, were getting a bit pissed off because I obviously wasn't making a name for myself in their eyes, so I went to work with my old man on the building site for a couple of months. And that was good fun. At the same time I was playing clubs in the evenings with a band called The Roosters. Brian Jones and Paul Jones were in the band before me but they'd both gone their separate ways – Paul with Manfred Mann and Brian with The Stones.

Did Casey Jones and The Engineers come next?

(Laughs.) Oh dear! Yeh. Didn't last long though. It got my chops together though. It was all good experience. The Mersey thing was just happening and to be in a group like Casey Jones and The Engineers, I mean, you got a few good gigs just because he was a Liverpudlian.

Local Boy Makes Good
The Yardbirds, 1963–5

Were you an original member of The Yardbirds?

No. They'd already been going a couple of months and they'd had a lead guitarist who'd quit, or they'd chucked him out, and just by word of mouth I got the job. Then they wanted to make a hit record and I wasn't ready for that at that time. I probably never have been unless it's on my terms. But they thought that if they changed what they wore and did more top forty-type material they would get a hit record, and that's just exactly when I left them. I played on the record ('For Your Love'/'Got To Hurry'), it was OK, but I could see it was a pop tune written for the purpose of getting into the charts and nothing else. I think I left after the session.

You were resident band at the Crawdaddy for a short while, weren't you?

Yeh ... for quite a while, on Sunday nights. Every Sunday night. We came straight in after The Stones, actually. A week after. They did it for almost a year, I think, and we did almost a year when we were there.

Did you ever see The Stones perform there?

I used to live there. It was incredible. It was better when they were playing there because they took half the crowd with them when they left, and it took us quite a while to build up our own sort of following. It was never really the same though. Obviously it wasn't the same for us anyway to be on stage after having been part of the audience.

Have you come across the sort of atmosphere that existed then since you left?

Well, I suppose so, but I always feel like an outsider. I've never had the same feeling of being in an audience as I did in those days, because I was younger and I knew all the people there. There was a crowd, a set, that used to go down there and everyone knew one another. I don't generally like being in audiences these days.

35

Were your friends at that time also musicians?

No, not really. Just loonies . . . you know. Just weekend ravers . . . dossers.

How did the 'guitar hero' element arise? It seems to me that you were the first musician in the pop/rock field to achieve fame on the basis of sheer musicianship rather than image?

You've got me there . . . I really have no idea. I pretended to take it in my stride. It must have surprised me really, but I tried to cover it.

Could you feel this hero worship building . . . for you as a guitarist?

I'll tell you what was going on. All the crowd that used to go to see The Stones were all my mates, so that when I joined The Yardbirds and we took over at the Crawdaddy I had my own fan club built in. A lot of them just used to come because they knew me, so I suppose that could have been the kick-off.

There was no precedent, though, was there for adulation of a musician for his musicianship in the rock field?

Well, I still don't think you could so much attribute it to the music as to camaraderie. I don't know what they saw in it, but it was just a 'local boy makes good' sort of thing.

Was that when the 'Slowhand' tag developed?

Giorgio Gomelski nicknamed me that in one of his witty moments. He ran the Crawdaddy Club and used to introduce me that way.

In much the same way as you're introduced on the 'Five Live Yardbirds' album?

Yeh. He was funny that bloke – Hamish Grimes – because if the audience weren't whipped up enough when The Stones were doing the Crawdaddy, he'd have this table by the stage and he'd get up on it and do this incredible go-go dancing! Sort of getting them at it and waving his arms in the air, and it sort of started up a dance. It was probably the original idiot dancing – everyone used to get up and wave their arms about and go into a frenzy, and he'd be the leader. It was really strange.

36

How do you explain the fact that, in the early sixties, a generation of essentially middle-aged white kids suddenly found an identity in a music that was rooted in a lower-class black culture?

Well, I can only speak for myself, and I always assumed that everyone who played blues in those days came from art school. It seemed to be something you learned in art school. As opposed to art, you learned how to play the blues. It was a very strange sort of side effect of being an art student, because everyone that I knew was either from an art college, going to an art college, or had been kicked out of an art college. They all seemed to have the same tastes and they were quite a cross-section of people – they weren't necessarily working class or middle class. They were from all kinds of families. A lot of them were from families that were having a hard time – either divorced or very strange domestic situations – and they probably didn't feel very welcome at home.

You really see that as something significant about your particular set of people?

A lot of people that were at art college were like that, yeh. I remember having the radio on when I was a little boy and there were certain things that mysteriously got played on 'Family Favourites'. Like you suddenly heard a Brownie McGhee and Sonny Terry record, or something like that, and it would just stick out like a sore thumb. You couldn't exactly explain why but it hit something inside, and I never really discovered what it was until years later. I didn't know what the name of the record was or anything, but I just heard this sound and then, when I finally began to look around, I saw that that was what it was . . . but I couldn't have explained then.

How do you mean 'What it was'?

Well, I heard the record again years later and realised that it was a blues record, but I didn't know that at the time. I didn't know what category it was from.

Did you have a particularly unhappy childhood?

No. I think I had quite the opposite. I think I had a very good time, really. I mean, it was on the cards that I wouldn't have because of the strange family set-up I was in. I could have made the worst of it

37

and had a really bad time, and I have often been told that I was a nasty kid, but I definitely had a lovely time growing up.

So you didn't seek consolation in music?

Not consciously, no. I probably do now, and the fact that I do must come from somewhere. It probably did but I didn't realise it. I don't actually remember being in a depressed state though and thinking 'Oh, I'll go and put a record on or listen to the radio.'

How big an influence do you think the early sixties British art-school scene has been on rock music?

I don't think it was a big influence. I think it just controlled a small corner of what was going on. Most of what gets into the charts has nothing at all to do with that sort of influence. It's much more just straight commercial music. The art college people are really outnumbered in that respect.

But if you take the biggest rock bands of the last decade – The Beatles, The Stones, Cream, The Who, The Kinks, Led Zeppelin – you find they've all got ex-art school people in them.

That's just to name a few, but there are thousands of other bands that have never had any of their members attend an art school and they're just as important in influencing the music scene. It'd be a bit boring if all the bands had the same sort of quality.

But there are innovative bands and imitative bands, and often it's a handful of the first type of band that allow for the possibility of thousands of the second type.

You could say, I suppose, that art schools do breed a certain kind of innovation in musicians. It's all mysterious! I'm not sure that I've got an objective point of view on the subject. It doesn't seem to be like that any more though. I mean, those people you mentioned are still around and they're still making it. It's not going on in the art schools any more.

When The Yardbirds toured with Sonny Boy Williamson in 1963, were you overawed by him?

Yeh, he was quite frightening actually because you never knew when he was being serious or not. He used to threaten you with the most awful things if you didn't do what he wanted.

38

How did that affect your playing?

We did what he said! It was exciting really, because he made you do things that you probably would have liked to have done and musically would have come around to doing, but they were also things that you would have been frightened to try out on your own. He just used to get you to do it there in front of him until it was right and he approved. It was the kind of thing where you thought at the time, 'Oh, fuck . . . I don't want to do this. I don't. Why should I be taking orders?' And then, when you'd finally got it together, you thought, 'Oh . . . it sounds good. I wish I had thought of that myself.' But he was a very powerful character.

So it was a good period of learning?

Yeh, because when he was with us we never used to do any of our own stuff – maybe one number before he came on – so we were just his backing band and we really had to learn to play his way. I haven't really heard any of that stuff since then properly, but I should imagine it was a fairly cooking little combo, as they say. He had a very set act – he did it the same way every night and it had to be just right. I mean, he was allowed to get pissed out of his head and do whatever he wanted. There was one night at Fairfields Halls in Croydon where we were all on stage with the lights out, and there was this curtain to the side where he was to walk through and the spotlight would hit him as he came across the stage . . . and this night they announced 'And now . . . Sonny Boy Williamson', and this figure collapsed through the curtain and all these harmonicas fell out of his coat or somewhere. About twenty harmonicas! And he just lay there in a heap and the spotlight hit him. We just didn't know what to do. He couldn't get up or anything – he had to be dragged off to the dressing room and then they cancelled the gig. Another thing he'd do would be to collapse into the drum-kit if he leant back too far. But he used to consume a bottle of Scotch in a day without blinking.

Was B. B. King a big influence on your playing at that time?

Always was in those days, yeh. Not as much as Freddie King, I don't think, because Freddie always had a funkier style of playing. B.B. was always clean – Freddie always had that distorted style even right at the beginning.

39

Do you think it's best for a developing artist to begin by conscious imitation or try to create something unique right from the word go?

Well . . . it's a gamble either way. You just have to pick which is the best way. You have to follow your nose. I mean, if you really like someone you copy him because you can't help it.

You want to do to others what he does to you?

Well exactly, yeh. But some people, who've probably got stronger determination to make it and actually have their own ideas, must just think, 'Well, fuck it! I'm not going to imitate anyone.' They've got big enough egos to want to push their own ideas even if they're not any good, and sometimes that pays off even more.

You left The Yardbirds over the 'commercial' aspect, didn't you?

Well . . . it was a grudge I suppose because . . . well, it was a combination of things really. It stemmed from the fact that Giorgio, or maybe it was even us, decided that we were going to have a hit single, and everyone started to contribute ideas of what they thought was going to be a good hit single. It finally came down to a split choice as to whether we did this Graham Gouldman song 'For Your Love', which was Paul Samwell-Smith's idea, or this Otis Redding song which was my idea. I'd never heard of Otis before and I'd just got this one single which Giorgio had given me and I wanted to do that. So, it came down to, 'Well, Sam can produce his and you can produce the Otis Redding one and then we can decide.' Well, Sam did his first and everyone just said 'Oh, that's it. No need to try yours.' So I thought, 'Fucking hell!' and I got really upset and bore a grudge, and I think that when they said it I actually made up my mind that I wasn't going to play with them any more. It was like kids, you know.

You never regretted it then?

Thankfully, no. I could have done because it was a spiteful decision and it was done out of temper and tantrum. Often you regret that sort of decision, but I don't think I ever did because it worked out well with me getting into John Mayall shortly after that, which was better for me.

Did Giorgio want to take The Yardbirds and put them on The Stones level? Was that the idea?

I think so, because he was always pretty cheesed off that The Stones had eluded him as far as management was concerned. You see, the funny thing about Giorgio is that he's so soft and malleable and he thought, 'Well, I'm not going to be like all these other managers and rip off my artists,' so he did a sort of hand-shake deal and he trusted them implicitly. Of course they weren't plotting against him or anything like that, but it was just that Andrew Oldham came along and spotted them and just snatched them away before Giorgio knew what was happening. Then I think he thought, 'Well, if that's how tough it's going to be I'd better actually sign up a group.' Even then when I left, it was no big deal. He could have slapped something on me. I think I did sign some kind of contract and he could have really made it tough for me, but he didn't. He just said 'OK'.

I get the impression that the playing was a bit muffled on the 'Five Live Yardbirds' album.

That recording's pretty poor. The circumstances weren't very good for recording, but the Mayall album was done by Mike Vernon and he was really shit hot. He just knew what the sounds should be like. He'd been a blues collector for a long long time and he knew exactly what a blues band should sound like.

Let My Guitar Sing to You
Learning, Playing, Writing

Can you remember particular records that you learned from or records that you used to play along to?

Yeh. Very early on I think I consciously tried to play along with all the Big Bill Broonzy records I had. I learned 'pieces', because he had quite a few instrumentals that were pretty simple once you knew where he was coming from and how he was approaching it and what key it was in. You could actually get it off and do it exactly the same. That was right at the beginning when I started to play, and after that I never really copied anyone quite as much. When I started playing electric guitar it was a different style and you didn't need to play as much, so you were freer to explore for yourself.

You started out with an acoustic guitar?

Yeh.

You never played along to Freddie King records then?

I played along with them but his kind of playing was much more abstract after the Broonzy stuff and things like that, which were more like rags and pieces which repeated themselves and were easy to learn once you'd got the knack. But imitating a Freddie or B. B. King solo was much harder because it required more finesse to actually copy it note for note, so it wasn't really worth trying once you'd found that out.

So how did you achieve that style of playing?

Well, I just tried to pick up the feeling or the sound.

Did you do that by changing your guitar?

Yeh . . . well, changing guitars in terms of going to an electric from an acoustic.

But how much of it was down to strings and other purely material things?

In those days a lot because you didn't really know what they were

42

doing. You didn't know how they achieved it, so obviously you explored all the different ways in which they could have done it like using really light gauge strings or really sensitive pick-ups or whatever. But when I met B. B. King for the first time and discovered that he was using really standard medium gauge strings or heavy gauge strings, that was way off mark because I was trying to do it the easy way whereas he'd been doing it the way that was most natural to him.

The materials must be important though because if you've got a really bum guitar with really bum strings. . . .

Yeh . . . yeh, but it depends on the player because some people can have the best start in the world and get nowhere and others can play on something you can get from Woolworths and make it sound a dream. It's possible.

Are you one of these people?

No. I don't think so.

I read somewhere that you used to practise obsessively 'sometimes locking himself away for weeks at a time just to perfect a riff'.

Nonsense. Absolute nonsense. I can't ever remember doing that. I've always liked to play with records but I've never really treated it as a study. I couldn't do it in order to educate myself or just as a personal exercise. It was always entertainment for me and nothing else.

Has that been obsessive?

Yeh. I do obsessively entertain myself. I mean, I start to put records on from the minute I get up . . . no matter what I'm doing.

Have you ever heard a riff and spent hours until you've been able to absolutely get it off?

Yeh. On the odd occasion.

But the weeks locked away are someone else's fantasy?

Definitely. I just can't remember me ever doing that . . . unless I was forced to because I had no one to talk to or I couldn't get out or something like that.

Do you ever practise now?

I practise at the last minute if I've got a gig or if I'm going to do a session, and it's absolutely necessary because your fingers get soft at the tips unless you play a bit now and then. Now I only play really when I'm trying to formulate a song or an idea ... trying to achieve something. I still don't do it as an exercise.

How do you formulate a song?

How do you formulate a song? You don't really. You just play around on the guitar and it formulates itself.

And the words come simultaneously

Yeh, they usually come from sound. I mean, you can just hum and then you find you're humming certain syllables which are pretty close to words as they are. You just have to put vowels on the ends. I like writing songs where I can say something without saying very much at all.

Why's that?

Because I don't feel I've got a lot of important things to say. I think that unless you've got something important to say it's best to keep your mouth shut. So if I do write a song and I think it's going to have to have words rather than just humming, then I try and make it say as little as possible.

Do you try and say enough to get people scrambling for interpretations?

No. I don't consciously attempt to do anything for anybody else.

Would you sing a telephone directory?

Probably not because what my lyrics usually come from are actual phonetics – words that have appealing sounds or sets of words. Like 'Night after day' (Opposites) is i, $\bar{a}$, $\bar{e}i$ ... you know. It comes out of humming.

But take a song like 'Give Me Strength'. It seems to have more to it than just sounds.

Yeh, yeh. Well, it's pretty easy to write a song like that because you're not writing anything brand new. It could have been sung by anybody. There's nothing really innovative about those words. I mean, 'Dear Lord, give me strength' – people say that just walking around the street. People say it in exasperation, 'Dear Lord! Give me strength!'

But knowing what you were going through at the time of writing, the song takes on a lot more.
That's just your interpretation, because you know.

But aren't I right in saying that?
Yeh.

It was after you'd come off heroin. Just after the treatment?
Yeh.

It seems to me that you can never remove a song from the context of the person who wrote it and the circumstances surrounding it's writing.
Well, having known me it would be pretty hard, but if you don't know me you'd just have to take the song on face value really.

Would you say that anything significantly changed your guitar sound? I'm meaning the actual sound now rather than the playing. For instance, the thick sound you obtained with Cream.
Well, that came out of using a lot of amps and being very loud. If you want to play to a large audience and you've got a very big amp with everything turned up full, you'd get a very very raucous sound. I always attempted to get a lot of volume but to take as much edge off it as I could so that it was round and not harsh. You could then still listen to it without it hurting your ears. That was the birth of a sound in a way, which I then carried on using over and over again because I liked the sound.

When did you first use a wah-wah pedal?
In Cream – on a track called 'Tales Of Brave Ulysses'.

Were they in use before that?
Someone's actually said that someone used a wah-wah in 1948, a very primitive kind of thing, and that's possibly so but I'd never heard of one before. It was just that I was in New York and went to a shop called Manny's, where they always have new gadgets and things, and they showed me this thing and I thought it was amazing so I just used it on that session. I thought I was the first person ever to use one but . . . there's always someone else who's done it!

Did you get into any other gadgets?

No, I never did really. No, the only thing I like using still is a wah-wah. I can't handle anything else. I've got too simplistic a nature really to be able to involve it. I know some people who have a whole line or maybe six or seven foot pedals next to one another that can do just amazing things – make it sound like a flute, give it echo, wah-wah, phasing – but I can't handle that many choices.

When I read recently that Charlie Parker attempted to translate the agility of a clarinet to the alto sax, it got me thinking about your own playing and I wondered whether you'd ever tried to make your guitar do a similar translation for the harmonica?

What made you think of that?

I think both reading the book and listening to a lot of the albums in your collection – many of which feature harmonica over guitar.

Well, I tell you what – on a harmonica, because it's your breath, you can hold a note. You can blow a note and hold it, bend it and do all kinds of things which people never really did with guitars for a long time. So, once that feedback thing made it possible for you to control and hold a note for as long as you wanted, it naturally began to sound like a harmonica. Then you located yourself with someone good like Little Walter or Jimmy Cotton and thought, 'Well, if I can play those long notes then I can learn some of their licks.'

Did you do that?

Yeh, yeh. I used to get off as many as I could because then people wouldn't be able to spot them and say, 'Ah well, he copped that from Freddie King' because they wouldn't be thinking 'Ah, he copped that from Little Walter.'

I was reading a review recently that said that Townshend was rhythmic, Page was sonic, Hendrix was funky and you were lyrical. How does that sound?

Very very generalised. What's sonic?

Dealing principally in sounds. Page is more concerned with the sound whereas I would agree that your playing is more lyrical.

I think we all tried to cover all of those things – some more success-fully than others. Actually that's quite close, except that I think

Jimi had them all covered. He could go from one thing to another and just have it perfectly covered.

I read in Curtis Knight's book on Hendrix that you and Townshend used to turn up regularly at his gigs and Townshend is quoted as saying 'Eric was one side of the coin and I was the other and we used to go and watch Jimi who was like an embodiment of the two styles that we had.' I assumed from this that he was meaning the rhythmic and lyrical qualities.

Well, he probably didn't mean it as specifically as that. He meant all that we'd like to do in any field on the guitar. What we were stretching to do then, Pete in his way and I in mine, and then to walk into a club and see someone that you'd never seen before who'd got it covered . . . ! You see, we thought that we must be ahead of everyone else, so that if anyone's trying to do what we're doing they're nowhere near as good as we are at doing it. And then to have Jimi lay all that down was quite heavy!

How did you feel?

Shattered and very very pleased. It was a great relief that someone had got there.

Did it make it all seem possible?

It seemed impossible for you, but possible at the same time because someone had got there and therefore it was attainable.

Have you played with B.B. and Freddie King?

Yeh. I've played with B.B. I think it was the second time I met him in the Village in New York and he was doing a club gig where I went down and we were introduced and he seemed to know of me, which was nice. We sat down and jammed for hours and it was recorded. I don't know what ever happened to the tapes. Freddie I played with on a couple of occasions on the last tour where he came on three or four dates with us and would come on as the encore act and we'd do a big blues number. It was really quite something.

Does he ever comment on your playing?

No. He's pretty much of a stud. He's not about to be diplomatic and sort of friendly. He loves it, he loves it all, but he's his own

47

man and he's not about to say that you're good or anywhere as near as good as he is. Just, 'Yeh . . . you can play good.'

Taking that he's been around a lot longer than you have and that you've been influenced by his playing, where would you say he's gone off or you've diverged?

He's been playing the same thing all that time. That's the funny thing about Freddie even more so than B.B. because B.B. has gone into different bags with strings and all kinds of things whereas Freddie never has. He's always been playing exactly the same way and probably not really advanced his style of playing much more in the last fifteen years. He's neither improved nor gone downhill. It's just straight ahead.

For yourself, you consciously want to advance your playing?

One of the things you'll probably find from all these interviews is that something inside me always wants to go somewhere else. It never gets settled down anywhere and it would be nice if it wasn't like that. I do admire someone like Freddie; I know him now and I'll go back and play with him in ten years time and he'll be exactly the same. Just the same straight-ahead drive. I might not even be playing anything.

It struck me the other day that you've had relationships with quite a few poets over the years. You lived with Ted Milton. Pete Brown wrote the lyrics for Cream and you were closely associated with Martin Sharp. Then I remember quite a time ago reading an interview with a poet where he said, 'Well, personally I'd rather be Eric Clapton' meaning, I suppose, I'm only writing poetry because I can't play guitar. Then reading Rolling Stone's *review of 'The History of Eric Clapton', I see that the reviewer quotes a friend of his saying, 'If there are poets of the guitar Clapton is one.' Now your playing revolves very much around feeling, putting feeling into sound. All people have the feelings you put into sound, the feelings aren't exclusive to you, but the ability to translate them into sound is. In the same way, I think, a poet takes the feelings everybody has and has the ability to translate them into words. If you took this to be true, would you say it was a fair assessment of what you're doing?*

Yeh, very good.

A poet of the guitar!

Yeh, I think that's a pretty interesting way of looking at it really. I could never do it with words because words always come to me as sounds; I could never get involved in making them mean anything rather than what they sounded like. Bob Marley . . . now he writes phonetically. It's almost like that idiot language that they dreamed up for backward kids who couldn't read or write. It was all phonetics and it was amazing. I tell you, if you get used to hearing words and not reading them very much, if you get used to hearing them as phonetic sounds, then when you get words that really do mean something or that are heavy they're twice as heavy because you've just been hearing words as sort of childish noises. So when you read a few that put you in your place, you get taken aback because words don't generally mean much to you.

Do you think we're entering a non-literate generation?

It's possible, isn't it? It's possible, because with everything becoming so intense I often notice when someone loses their temper the way they shout doesn't involve using words at all. It could be just gibberish or anything . . . it's just the sounds they make.

Hendrix once said that people were now disillusioned with politics and were turning to music because 'Music never lies. It can be misinterpreted but it never lies.'

You can't make music lie. It's either in tune or not. It's either appealing to you or it isn't.

It's a bad word to have used because for a lie to exist you have to have an absolute standard of truth by which the statement can be judged. This doesn't exist in music. If you put your guitar out of tune and play because that's what you want to play, then that's truth I suppose.

Well, you can't even do that because it's offensive to the ears. You can disguise a lie when you tell it to someone, but you can't musically unless you put words into it and use music to tell a lie. It's not often that's done.

For all the talk about 'poetry in rock', outside of Dylan and a handful of others, there hasn't been a lot of quality lyric. And yet, maybe the real poetry is in the musical translation of feeling?

I found that with Dylan. People I used to live with liked Dylan not for the music but just for the words, just for what he was saying. At that time, which was before 'Just Like A Rolling Stone' came out, I was finding it very difficult to see it from their point of view at all because there wasn't enough music content or feeling in the music, which was very skiffly and buskish. I couldn't really latch on to it until he got into some nice rock things where I could listen to it without actually getting involved in what he was saying. The whole 'Blonde On Blonde' album was perfect, a good combination. Then he blended the words just right with the music. They were more abstract and became phonetically easier to listen to in the same way that the music has matured. There's no dynamics in 'Blood On The Tracks' . . . it's that sort of line-up all the way through and it's played exactly the same way. There's no lift.

What was your first lyric?
'Presence Of The Lord'.

You've got into lyrics since then?
Not really.

You did most of the 'Layla' album?
Yeh . . . that was all me, I suppose. I still don't find it easy. I don't find it enjoyable because I still find I'm inhibited by rhyme as much as anything else. I'll write out a verse, and I'll get hung up on one word, maybe it's not even a word that had to rhyme, just one word that you could use twenty other words in place of it that would sound better but wouldn't mean the same thing. I think I'm in a difficult position to write words because I feel I have a responsibility to make it all sound good as much as mean something, whereas a real lyric writer will just write out good lyrics without giving a fuck about what they sound like. Then someone else can put the music to it. I'm sure that Bernie Taupin is a natural lyric writer because phonetically his lyrics do sound good when they're put to music. Someone like that is a gem because I'm sure he doesn't write with music in his head. He just writes down the words and they work. When I'm writing a song, I'm writing the lyrics and trying to think how they're going to fit musically, how they'll sound.

Do you still enjoy session work?
Yeh. I did much more session work when I was younger because

there was less competition around. Now when I go into a studio and cut a session I've really got to work hard to keep my head above water when there's so many other good young players about. I don't feel threatened as much as I feel 'Why should I do it if there's someone who can do it better?' I don't sit there and fear. That's how I'd feel if I was threatened – I'd feel frightened. I just feel pressured to do better than I've been doing – to keep improving.

My Purist Number
John Mayall's Bluesbreakers, 1965

Did Mayall ask you to join The Bluesbreakers?

Yeh. He called me up about two weeks after I'd left The Yardbirds
... because of that article in *Rave*. I suppose he'd seen that. It
suited me fine because it was a blues band and I was going through
my purist number then. For me, in those days, blues was the only
kind of music and I didn't like anything else.

Was that a significant article for you then?

Yeh ... it was the first time I'd ever got any individual press
coverage.

*You were quoted in it as saying, 'For me to face myself I have to play
what I believe is pure and sincere and uncorrupted music. That is why
I had to leave.'*

Big words!

*Well, it was that type of magazine at that time. It was all down to
favourite colours and ideal girl-friends.*

Yeh ... I suppose so.

Had you heard The Bluesbreakers play before you joined them?

Yeh, come to think of it I had. They'd had a pretty big hit record
'Life Is Like A Slow Train Crawling Up A Hill' which actually
caught on in America. I'd seen them on gigs too. I'd seen them at
The Flamingo. I wasn't that keen on them because I never really
thought that John had a lot of control over his voice. He seemed to
know what he wanted to do but not exactly how he wanted to do it.
But, I mean, there were very few people around that could do anything properly. It was all very rough in those days, wasn't it?
Except for maybe Georgie Fame who had what he was doing
together, but most people were imitating other people pretty poorly.

*I hear that you split from Mayall at one point and went off to Greece
with a carload of musicians?*

Yeh. My little crowd of mates that I was with decided one day that we were going to take a band round the world. I was the only one who was playing professionally and the rest of them were doing other things to make a scratch. There was Ben, who played piano and was a wood carver, and Bernie, who was a doctor playing saxophone. Then there was John Bailey, who was studying Kinetics or Physics at university, and he was the singer. That was the band! A really crazy band! We used to live at Ted Milton's house, you know – the poet and puppeteer extraordinaire. They were wino days. Everyone was drinking wine by the gallon and getting wiped at three o'clock in the afternoon. Anyway, we only got as far as Greece where we played in a club. The night we started playing the Greek band, whose interval we were playing in, got into a road accident and three of them were killed. I immediately offered to deputise and so I was playing something like twelve hours on the trot, because when my band went off they came on and I just stayed on stage. I had to learn all The Kinks' numbers and Beatles' tunes and everything. Then the owner of the club took a liking to me and said that I should stay and be the guitarist with the group. So I actually had to escape, and I lost an amp which I left in the club because they're really violent people if they think you're going to double-cross them. I had a mad dash to the station where I caught the Orient Express and came back home.

Was this all of you?

No, just me and the piano player. Two of them carried on in that same car and actually got all the way around the world. They went to Australia and back up through the Americas.

What made you leave what seemed to be an ideal band – judging from what you said you wanted to be involved in on leaving The Yardbirds – to embark on a self-arranged world tour with a bunch of amateur musicians?

Well, it really wasn't that ideal. No band is that ideal to be in. Always after a little while you start to find things that you're slightly ashamed of being in the band for – I mean, just quirks. John has many quirks, believe me. Bands, when they've got a leader, often gang up against him behind his back and in The Bluesbreakers we used to really take the piss out of him behind his back on stage.

Was your relationship with Mayall very strong?

Pretty strong. I used to live at his house for a long time in a room that was like a cupboard. He was amazing, man. I mean, no one was allowed to drink! John McVie got slung out of the band wagon half-way between Birmingham and London one night because he was drunk and he had to make his own way home. Also, he had his own bunk bed in the van did John, and you had to sit upright in the front while he got into bed in the back. And if we did a gig in Manchester where his parents lived he'd go and stay the night at his mum's and we'd have to sleep in the van. He didn't get you a hotel or anything. So there were those disadvantages being in that band! It wasn't all roses. Again . . . there were some very strong rumours that he'd inherited a million. I don't know whether it was true, but that's what we always used to say about him.

Musically were you happy with that band?

Most of the time, yeh. It seemed to be the only thing worth doing at the time.

Did you have that copy of The Beano comic with you at the time the cover photograph was taken on The Bluesbreakers album, or was it set up?

Oh. It was very early in the morning. I don't know what that's got to do with it! I was sleepy-eyed and didn't know what to do so I went and bought a *Beano*. I did used to like *The Beano* in those days though. I thought they were quite funny. Desperate Dan was good. I could never figure out how a cowboy could be in the middle of somewhere like Liverpool . . . you know what I mean? Because there were street lamps and buses everywhere and things like that.

Was it around this time that the 'Clapton is God' wall writings began appearing?

With John Mayall? Yeh . . . it was. You know what it was? Some journalist said that he'd seen a kid writing it on the wall and yet it's never necessarily been true. The bloke probably never saw anyone doing that, but by putting it into print he made it the thing to do for a little while.

Was working with Mayall a big musical freedom for you coming after your time with The Yardbirds?

Yeh. It was, but then this Greek expedition was an even bigger freedom because it was all my mates – that was why I wanted to do it. I mean, although we weren't a shit hot band we played exactly what we felt like playing and had a good time as well because there was no back-biting.

How did the Mayall thing end then?

Well, I returned from Greece and picked up with John where I'd left off. I think I'd told him that I did want to come back to the band, that I just wanted this working holiday, and so he got Pete Green in, I think, while I left and took me back in when I got back. But I was still never very settled there. I was always looking for somewhere else and then I started to formulate ideas about getting together with Jack and Ginger. I tell a lie – Ginger had the idea. It was a sort of mystical experience because I think I had thought about it and then Ginger came to a gig and suggested it.

You mean that he'd thought about you and Jack?

No . . . he didn't necessarily include Jack in it because he'd had that bad experience with him in Graham Bond. I think they nearly killed each other on stage or something. They've both got different versions of the story but it seems that one of them called the other a cunt or something and the other punched him and the other went mad because they've both got furious tempers. So that was always just on the boil the whole time with the Cream. It was just ready to explode and anything would get it going. I wasn't really old enough or experienced enough to sort it out. I just used to get it out of the way if I could.

A Few Good Licks
Cream, 1966–8

Was the formation of Cream at all influenced by the Jimi Hendrix Experience?

No. We'd been going about two weeks when he came to England. I remember Chas (Chandler) brought him to one of our gigs. We were playing somewhere in London and we jammed and I thought, 'My God!' I couldn't believe it! It really blew my mind. Totally. And then he got a three-piece together.

How did all this affect your music?

It opened it up a lot because I was still at that time pretty uptight by the fact that we weren't playing one hundred per cent blues numbers, and to see Jimi play that way I just thought, Wow! – that's alright with me! It just sort of opened my mind up to listening to a lot of other things and playing a lot of other things. Jimi and I always had a friendship from a distance because we never really spent a lot of time together, only during the acid period I used to see him a lot. Occasionally we'd spend time alone together just raving about but, I mean, it was always a distant friendship. Playing together was something else.

How did the volume thing come about?

I suppose because it was a three-piece and we were playing larger gigs; I think all of us at the same time thought being a three-piece wasn't enough and that we had to compensate by playing loud. That, and also in order to get feedback and stuff like that. To feel it going through your body was exhausting though. It was just like going and working out in a gym to play that loud.

Do you think press reaction affected Cream in the end?

Do you really want me to bring that up? You see, there was a constant battle between Jack and Ginger because they loved one another's playing and couldn't stand one another's sight. I was the mediator and I was getting tired of that, and then this *Rolling Stone* came out with an interview with me boosting my ego followed on the next page by a concert review deflating it, calling me 'the master of the cliche', which knocked me cold. At that point in time I decided that I was leaving Cream. Also, another interesting factor was that I got the tapes of 'Music From Big Pink' and I thought, well, this is what I want to play, not extended solos and maestro bullshit but just good funky songs. The combination of that *Rolling Stone* thing and hearing 'Big Pink' decided for me that I was going to split Cream.

What about the fact that, as you've already told me, the audiences were responding to music which you weren't happy with? Where does that come in?

Well, once we'd got our wings we couldn't play a note wrong. I thought, this isn't right because the music we're playing is useless. OK, it had it's moments but it's not what they deserve. They're paying too much, they're applauding too much and it makes me feel like a con man. I don't want to feel like a con man. I want to feel that I've earned what I've got. You see it got to the point where we were playing so badly and the audience were still going raving mad – they thought it was a gas. But I thought, we're conning them, we're cheating them. We're taking their bread and playing them shit. I can't work on that basis.

How early on in the Cream's existence were you dissatisfied?

After the Fillmore (1967) we did a tour that went on for five months – one-nighters. That did me in completely. I just experimented one night – I stopped playing half-way through a number and the other two didn't notice, you know! I just stood there and watched and they carried on playing 'til the end of the number. I thought, well fuck that, you know! You see, Cream was originally meant to be a blues trio, like Buddy Guy with a rhythm section. I wanted to be Buddy Guy, the guitarist with a good rhythm section.

What sort of gigs did you intend to play?

Small clubs. We didn't want to be big in any way.

When did you realise things weren't turning out this way?

The Windsor Jazz and Blues Festival 1966, which was almost our first gig. We found that we ran out of numbers so quickly that we just had to improvise. So we just made up twelve-bar blues and that became Cream. That became what we were known for. I liked it up to a point, but it wasn't what I wanted.

Why did you release 'Wrapping Paper' as your first single when it was so un-Cream and un-blues?

Well, another idea we had with Cream was to be totally dada and have weird things on-stage and stuff like that. It never really happened but 'Wrapping Paper', I suppose, was part of that kind of attitude. You know – put out something weird!

What had you thought Cream could do for you that The Bluesbreakers and The Yardbirds hadn't done?

I suppose I wanted to be a star. Not just a star, but a star doing what I would like to do. I still thought in terms of playing straight blues or rock blues but being a star on the strength of that and not on commercially inclined music.

What did you think constituted a star?

Popularity.

In terms of recognition for what you were doing or affection from a large proportion of the public?

A combination of the two I suppose. A crusade for that type of music combined with the need to be in the spotlight.

Do you still feel that way?

Yeh. I love the spotlight.

Has it never disillusioned you?

Yeh ... a bit when I had my eye trouble in America. I had conjunctivitus and couldn't fucking see. My eyes were literally just big red puffy slits and I'd get this incredible white light on me which I usually love and tears would pour down my face. It was horrible. It's not intellectual disillusionment but physical disillusionment.

Yeh ... but what I was meaning was ...

I know (laughter). It was just that I thought I could get out of it! (laughter).

What advantage have you got over me?

I can walk on stage and stand in the spotlight and everyone will clap. You can't.

Is that the biggest part of being a star then?

One of the biggest parts, yeh. If you can build up that kind of enthusiasm without actually doing anything then you can do whatever you like on top of it. If you can walk out on stage and the audience is already with you you can do a lot wrong, but you can do a lot more wrong if they're not with you.

But you told me that one of the reasons you became disillusioned with Cream was precisely that. People were clapping bad work and you realised that they'd thrown out all discrimination.

I didn't value it as much then because the balance was all wrong. It was too much enthusiasm for too little music, too little real value.

Another thing – you're always taking risks with your albums. You never seem to use the appreciation that builds up for one particular album to sell the next one. There's absolutely no guarantee, for instance, that someone liking 'Layla' will like '461 Ocean Boulevard' is there?

I know. It's like seeing how much you can get away with. I don't deliberately set out to make a bad album but I know when I've done something that isn't up to par. I know some things on the new album ('One In Every Crowd') which really aren't that good at all and they'll be discovered in reviews and such like and after a few plays people will hear it. But perhaps that's just because I'm getting old. I mean, when I was listening to my solo album last night ('Eric Clapton'), I was even considering that that might have been my peak and I used to think that 'Layla' was. I was thinking last night that perhaps that was my peak, perhaps now I'm going downhill. You never really know. You can't tell until you look back over a whole career. In retrospect you can get a better idea.

How do you view the Bowie 'experiment' with stardom – the conscious attempt to be a star and play with the whole mechanics of stardom to prove that it can be done in two years?

Great. I think it's pretty good. I think if you've got good enough theatrical feel for what you can do and what you can't do you're probably going to end up with something incredibly good. I'm sure he knows by now exactly where the limits are before he reaches the shock value thing where people become disgusted. I'm sure he knows how far he can go.

Cream started as a blues-based trio, but had the acid thing come along at that point?

No. 1967 was when I had my hair permed and that was acid and when I first met George (Harrison) and John (Lennon). They were tripping about a lot.

Can you remember first taking acid?

The first time. Yeh . . . it was when we did the cover for 'Disraeli Gears' and we went up to Scotland and we took it at the bottom of Ben Nevis and then went up to the top. It was amazing. We ran down! Have you ever tried running down a mountain? You see, Ben Nevis is not steep because you've got this spiral path which goes all the way to the top and it's about a five-mile walk. It took us about half a day to get to the top and then about three hours to run down. You know, it was that kind of running where you can't stop . . . you've just got to make the best of it.

You were trying to decelerate?

No. Accelerate! We were on acid!

Can you still remember the whole feeling?

Great. Incredible feeling. As a matter of fact I didn't trip that much; I only ever had one bad trip and it wasn't extremely bad – I just thought I was going to die. But, I mean, it was all right because I thought, well, if I'm going to die it doesn't matter. I'll just go and lie somewhere. So I went into a room, lay down on a bed and waited to die. I can remember people coming in and saying, 'Are you all right?' and me saying, 'Oh yes. Leave me alone. I'm dying.' It wasn't that bad at the time. It was just the expectation of dying.

Who did the 'Disraeli Gears' cover then?

Martin Sharp. He wrote 'Tales Of Brave Ulysses'. He used to live with me at The Pheasantry in Kings Road. We actually met in The Speakeasy and became instant pals and leased this place together and lived there for a while. He wrote poetry, he painted and did work for *OZ* magazine. There was a great community of Australians around at that time.

In a sense he pioneered this acid art in Britian, didn't he?

Yeh. I think he did. He did a lot of posters. He did one of Jimi with his guitar exploding. As a matter of fact he did acid for a while, but after three or four trips he tripped out for ever and didn't need to take any more because he'd come down where he wanted to be. The thing about acid is that you've really got to put all your trust in it because you don't know where you're going to come down after a trip. I mean, you can come down in a weird place where you don't want to be and never be able to get out of there again. He found where he wanted to be and stayed there. He has constantly been on a trip ever since.

Were there a lot of people like him – artists, designers, writers, poets – who were part of your crowd at that time?

Yeh. It was really nice, a nice little set. The Kings Road was really flourishing in those days. There were a lot of good people around then and the area wasn't being mobbed, it wasn't being over-populated . . . it was just right. It was mainly people who were into crafts of some kind – arts of some kind, or music, clothes.

Did you feel that the culture was moving together in a cohesion which has since been lost?

It was great. There was an incredible feeling of sort of everything coming together. Everyone was always saying that and going around saying 'Isn't it good how jazz and rock are fusing and how every-thing is meeting'. There did seem to be a big fusion of things at that time.

So how did acid affect what started out to be straight-ahead blues music?

Well . . . that could be it, couldn't it? You might have a point there.

Had you never considered that?

No. Oh dear. It wasn't till after we'd played a few times that we started taking it and we never just played straight blues. We actually started attempting to write things in the beginning and that's how

61

songs like 'NSU' and 'Sweet Wine' came about which you couldn't call straight blues. But, truthfully speaking, we weren't into those long solo things I suppose until acid. Perhaps that could have been the cause of that. Acid was conducive to exploring music. The thing about it was that it shook all your foundations away, so that after the first couple of times you just realised that everything you'd been using as guidelines up until that point were actually pretty flexible if you decided to question them, which acid obviously did. You could then apply that to music but it never actually got much more specific than that for me. I just knew that I was freer than I had thought I was before.

A big development I would have thought.

A big development in your mind. A big realisation. But putting that into practice is always a matter of playing it down because you've still got the same technique to express it with and the same instrument to cope with. It doesn't just suddenly explode into something else . . . you've still got to change the whole thing very gradually.

Well, do you think these covers ('Disraeli Gears' and 'Wheels Of Fire') are a visual representation of what's going on inside the albums?

(Laughter). Is that a joke? (Laughter.) I don't think they do actually. I think they over-estimate what's going on. It would be really incredible if you could listen to the music and see that.

I was going to ask you – I sit here and ask you all these questions about your music but do you ever think about your music in a similar sort of way? It just strikes me when you say 'I hadn't thought of that before.'

Yeh, but I very often get the wrong end of the stick if I'm just thinking about it without an outside point of view to help. I often only do realise things like that after they're suggested to me.

Was the groupie scene developing by the time Cream went to America?

Yeh. It was red hot. I first went there to do a Murray The K show with The Who and there were just tons of them around then. I mean, pretty ugly ones but some fair ones too. There were both ends really – horrible spotty scrubbers and really nice looking middle-class chicks. Or just nice chicks who didn't realise they were making themselves into groupies – they were pretty innocent.

62

Why is it that lead guitarists rate so highly amongst groupies?

Who knows? Some chicks have things for bass players and some for drummers. I don't think you can fairly say that more go for any one kind of musician than any other.

Why go for musicians?

They're sort of outlaws I suppose and the lifestyle is very attractive. They know in a way that they need not get involved, so if they're a particularly insecure type of chick and they don't want to risk an involved relationship they just want to get their rocks off and do whatever they want in one night and probably think they'll never see you again.

Did you ever feel sad for the girls?

Sometimes, yeh. There are some chicks around who really are fucked-up in their heads and as a result they probably were carrying on like that at the time, but afterwards they look back on it and they feel so ashamed that they don't feel they can lead a straight life with anyone. They probably think they're whores. But as a rule they're the most incredibly warm people. I mean, there are a few exceptions – chicks who are just out to be super-star groupies because it's become the in thing to do, but in the early days they were just chicks who wanted to look after you when you were in town. If making love to you was going to make you happy, they'd make love. If you were tired and didn't want to make it, they'd cook you a meal and make you feel at home. They really were 'ports of call'.

Didn't you have an ambition at one time to lay a thousand girls?

I think I've done that now. It was a childhood ambition. Well, I thought I'd missed out a great deal because I didn't know about the facts of life 'til I was nine and I thought everyone else had known them ever since they came out the womb. So I thought I'd really missed out. I thought things were going on all around me that I didn't know about and I made up my mind to do something about it. In fact I don't think that was the case at all. I don't think anyone knows that much about it until they're nine, ten or eleven, and some people don't know about it until they're fifty or something.

So you started on the long haul when you were nine?
Yeh, yeh. No looking back.

You once told me that all this led to disillusionment and you said you'd realised you could have settled down happily with any one of them.

Yeh. I could have done . . . if I'd known then what I know now. But I wasn't about to. I still think that if I lived all over again, I'd probably do exactly the same. Probably try to get in a few more.

You also told me that one idea for Cream had been to make it a 'silly band' springing surprises on people all the time.

Yeh, I know. It was going to be a Bonzo Dog Band for about two weeks but we didn't actually have that much of a sense of humour and we weren't clever enough to pull it off. We couldn't think anything up for an act. The Bonzo's were sensational. The best we came up with was just having stuffed animals with us up on stage. It was really half-hearted. For two gigs we had a stuffed gorilla. It just shows you that the whole thing with Cream came out of not knowing what we were going to do.

How did you first meet Robert (Stigwood)?

Through Ginger. Ginger had a contract with him with Graham Bond . . . well, maybe not a contract, he was just Ginger's agent. We were just looking around for someone to manage our affairs and it was a question of who we knew and I didn't know anybody. Jack Bruce had also been handled by Robert because he was with Graham Bond when Ginger was with him, and so we all just signed personal contracts with him. I don't think he was managing anyone else then. I mean he'd been in that kind of business for a long time. He'd made and lost a lot of money before I'd ever met him in different kinds of show-biz businesses. He'd run a modelling agency and things like that. If you get him going about old stories, he's a very good raconteur and he's had some incredible things that have happened to him in the past.

So he wasn't immensely successful when you met him?

No, actually he was just about breaking even and then Cream took off. He used all the money we made very quickly to set up a little web and then he got the Bee Gees back from Australia and it just started to grow from there. I think he's in pretty good shape at the moment.

19 *Left:* Ginger Baker and Jack Bruce with The Graham Bond Organisation, 1966, before joining Cream *left to right:* Dick Heckstall-Smith, Ginger Baker, Jack Bruce and Graham Bond 20 *Below:* Cream 1966 *left to right:* Eric, Ginger Baker and Jack Bruce

21, 22 *Far left top:* In the early days, Cream on 'Ready! Steady! Go!' 23 *Far left below:* Cream 1967—'We were pretty smart dressers in those days' 24 *Top left:* Jimi Hendrix— 'We jammed and I thought "My God!" I couldn't believe it!' 25 *Below left:* Cream 1967—'I thought that if I had hair like Hendrix, I'd probably be able to play like that as well'

26 *Above:* Rehearsal for Cream's final performance at the Royal Albert Hall 1968 27 *Top right:* Blind Faith at their debut performance *left to right:* Eric, Stevie Winwood, Ginger Baker and Rich Grech 28 *Below right:* The Blind Faith concert at Hyde Park, 7 June 1969— 'There are 36,000 people waiting there for what you're going to do'

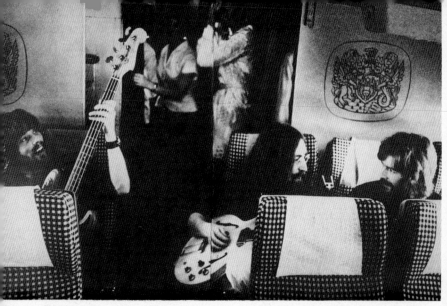

29 *Above:* En route to the concert for Peace in Toronto 1969—'While we were flying he (Lennon) told me what to do. I had to learn "Cold Turkey" and just sort of generally rehearse'

30 *Above:* George Harrison—'A very lively relationship...never boring'

31 *Above:* Producer Tom Dowd—'He's the King. He tells me when to stop and start and I take that as the law'

32 *Above:* Delaney and Bonnie with Eric—'Such down-home humble cats'

33 *Above:* Derek and The Dominos *left to right:* Jim Gordon, Carl Radle, Bonny Whitlock and Eric

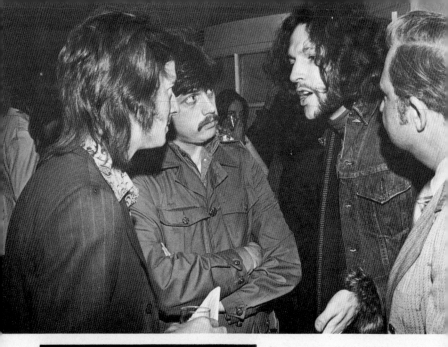

34 *Above:* Eric *(left)* with Christian DJ Scott Ross *(second from left)* 35 *Left:* Eric on stage in San Francisco

Is he really into your music?

As much as he's into anybody's music. I think he's really more a theatrical man than a music lover. He's got so many things going on at once that I don't know how he keeps it up. I couldn't handle it . . . getting up in the morning making phone calls and making deals every day. It's his gig though . . . it's what he does best. It tires him out. He can't relax. We went to Rio together for a holiday and he sat in his hotel room most of the day making business calls (laughs). It was supposed to be a really nice relaxed holiday and he was wound up.

What about 'Anyone For Tennis'? Was it written for a film?

Oh, don't. That's one of my . . . I hate that. It was embarrassing. Martin Sharp wrote the words. It was the other song he wrote. He wrote down the words and I didn't write the music until later. It was definitely a one-off shot because that song is the proof that that way of writing doesn't work for me. It worked just once with 'Tales Of Brave Ulysses' because the images were very powerful and you could not help but make good music around it, but 'Anyone For Tennis' was a bit spiky, pointing its finger a bit too much. A pretty, watery sort of protest song and as such it didn't inspire much musically. And I really worked on it for a long time trying to find the music that would make it right, but I just gave up and made the best of it in the end. Somehow, some people liked it, and they wanted to put it out as a single and someone used it for a film. But I find it really embarrassing to hear now.

You said that you'd never been happy with your performance with Cream although you'd got a couple of good licks in here and there.

With Cream we had our ups and downs. We had good gigs and bad gigs. We had gigs when you could have mistaken us for Hendrix, it was that good, and other times we were like the worst band in the world. It was this kind of inconsistency that relied upon the improvisation factor. All our songs had a starting theme, a finishing theme and a middle that was up to us. On a good night it was great and on a bad night it was awful. I couldn't take this kind of up and down. So I got in a few good licks while Cream was going. But like on 'Farewell' we did 'Badge' and I liked that. It was all because I played them 'Big Pink' and said, 'Look – this is what music is all about. Let's try and get a sound like this,' that we got the sound like 'Badge' and the rest. After I left Cream, let's see . . . what did I do? It was Blind Faith, wasn't it? Almost straight away?

Down-Home Humble Cats
Blind Faith/Delaney and Bonnie,
1969–70

So tell us about Blind Faith.

Well, I promised Ginger that whatever I did I'd take him with me because we had a close thing going. So, what happened was that we didn't rehearse enough, we didn't get to know each other enough, we didn't go through enough trials and tribulations before the big-time came. We went straight into the big gigs and I came off-stage at that Hyde Park concert shaking like a leaf because I felt once again that I'd let people down. There are 36,000 people waiting there for what you're going to do and if it's not what you think is right – no way! And then I met Delaney and Bonnie on the second night of the American tour and they were just such down-home humble cats and they were getting very little applause, very little money, and the only reason they were on the bill was because I'd asked for them to be the second act. So I started a rapport with Delaney, which became very strong and severed my relationship with Blind Faith. So, Blind Faith was breaking up in that Stevie and Ginger were arguing, Rick was kind of in the middle and I was out altogether. I was with Delaney and Bonnie. I already saw ahead that I didn't want Blind Faith. I wanted to be lead guitarist with Delaney and Bonnie because they were singing soul music.

Initially, what did you think you could have done with Blind Faith that you couldn't have done with Cream?

I didn't know. I never have that positive an idea of what direction I'm going in. I mean, I just thought 'Cream's got to go, but I still want to play,' and I'd always wanted to play with Stevie because I knew that he was a very laid-back musician.

So, ultimately, why didn't it work out?

Because we rehearsed for three weeks, publicised and all that hype, and the first audience we played to was 36,000 people at Hyde Park, London!

Why did you allow this to happen?

We had no control over it. We just sort of went along, we thought it would be all right. All the time we were touring, though, I was hanging out with Delaney and Bonnie because they were getting no money, bottom of the bill and no one was clapping them, and we were being adulated and all that rubbish and getting lots of bread. I think I did the right thing going off with them and stealing The Dominos away from them, you know. But the funny thing was that once I'd got 'Layla' out of my system, I didn't want to do any more with The Dominos. I didn't want to play another note.

How do you feel about 'Cream vacuum' bands such as Mountain and Grand Funk?

I think it's OK. I think that's great, you know. I mean, I'm honoured in a way that they felt like doing it that way. We must have done something good in order for them to want to carry it on. It relates in a way to people going around saying, 'Isn't it a drag that Jimi's dead. There'll never be another guitarist like him.' I turned on the radio in the car the other day and I thought 'That's weird, that's Jimi and I've never heard that track before,' and it turned out to be a guy called Robin Trower who used to play for Procol Harum. I mean, it's great. In a way Jimi's still alive because as long as you don't forget, you preserve. I must admit though I've never gone out of my way to listen to any of them. I'm very segregational like that. There are very few white bands whose records I'd actually buy. I like to listen to black music anyway. If I'd been introduced to their music by someone, if someone had played it to me and said 'Look, this is nice,' I'd listen to it. But if I walk into a record shop I know I always go for the blues rack or the soul rack, you know, not the heavy metal rack at all.

How did the 'Live Peace In Toronto' gig come about?

That's beyond me. John (Lennon) gets these things. I mean, he just sits there and thinks up these things to do that you wouldn't believe. I just had a phone call on the day we were to leave and he said that someone had asked him to do that concert and it was that night! So I had to make it to the airport in an hour, we went across on the plane and while we were flying he told me what he was going to do and he had a couple of songs like 'Cold Turkey' – I had to learn that, and just sort of generally rehearse.

You had to learn them on the plane?

Yeh. There weren't many people on it but it was still quite strange. Then we got off the plane and we were driven to the gig.

Were you happy with the performance?

Fucking good, yeh. I thought it was excellent because I'd played with him once before on The Stone's Circus but I hadn't a lot of experience playing with John; it was a thing that paid off, a blind faith thing that paid off. I like the album, I thought it was very good and I don't think that he'd entertained the idea of solo performances much before that.

Did you form particularly close relationships with The Beatles when they were . . . The Beatles?

With George – pretty instantaneously – we got on well and had a rapport going.

So you've been close friends ever since?

Yeh. Paul I never saw much of ever, still don't see much of. I think the first time I met John he was under the piano with Yoko. He was pretty detached at that time.

So recent developments haven't affected your relationship with George then?

Yeh. Put it in a very funny sort of light. I mean, we've had some really strange scenes recently. We bounce back and forth. I go over to his house sometimes and he ends up throwing me out and then he comes over here and ends up throwing himself out. It's still a very lively relationship. It's never boring. It's just become slightly freaky that's all.

What sort of relationship do you have with Pete Townshend?

Mutual respect I suppose. He's got a very serious attitude towards music. He can get as far out as anybody, he can keep up with Moon whatever Moon's up to but he's always very very serious about his music. He always comes back to that. He's got the dedication and nothing can throw him off once he's made his mind up to get on with something. You just can't get through to him.

Is Keith Richard a friend?

We used to hang out a lot in the early days. I used to go up to their flat in Chelsea and see them a lot. They were easy to get on with then because they were a bunch of mates. They weren't really sure what they were going to do more than anyone else was. I saw them quite a lot during that sort of period but then they got into the Chelsea hip crowd, which I did many years later I suppose. It's very tempting to become part of something which looks sort of exclusive.

You listened to the solo album last night and said that you really liked it. What was it about it that you liked in particular?

I think it was one of the best nuclei of musicians that ever got together. It was nice that it was captured on record and it's nice that it all came together to be my first solo album. It was like a little explosion, a little happening.

Was your writing with Delaney a distinct split between words and music?

It was pretty much Delaney. He's such an enthusiastic generous character and incredibly affectionate – if he becomes your buddy he's you bosom buddy. He's also ambitious too. A very strange combination. So, I mean, he'd sit down and write a song and tell you you'd written part of it! He'd write most of it and then say, 'Don't you remember that's the part you put in the other day.' If you thought about it you'd realise you hadn't actually done any of it, so it was kind of like he was giving you this song and also selling himself through it at the same time. I mean, I did actually put some of it together – a few words here, a few riffs there and a chord, but the main-stay was him.

Do you think the album broke new ground that you're building on now?

Yeh, but I don't think I really ever valued it rightly at the time. I never really did build properly on it because if I had I'd still be working with a band like that. I'd have horns and I'd have carried on with material like that and such like, but I didn't. I did actually take the nucleus of that band and make it into The Dominos, but it didn't sound the same. So I didn't really use it to its best advantage that album. Now, as I look back on it – it could have been a really good foundation for something. But you can't change what happened.

Were you asked to join The Stones when Brian Jones died?

Tentatively I think, yeh. But Mick never really gets to the point about things like that. He's very . . . you're supposed to pick up the hint and say, 'Well, what are you driving at?' and then he'll come out with it but I think I was forming either Blind Faith or The Dominos at the time.

They didn't try you this time when Mick Taylor left?

Hard to say. He (Mick Jagger) came to see me a lot in America and sort of would get very out of it and would talk about the good times we could have if things were different. He didn't ask me obviously or I'd know, but I think it might have crossed his mind.

Full Ahead
Derek and the Dominos,
1970–1

Why did you call the band Derek and The Dominos?

It was a joke. Tony Ashton suggested it because he always used to call me Del and he wanted to call it Del and The Dominos . . . so it became Derek and The Dominos. It was last minute, in the dressing room before we went on stage at The Lyceum. We didn't have a name up to that point. You don't think of that when you're forming a group. In fact, when someone suggests to you that you get a band title that's when you really start to worry about whether you should have a band at all, because you realise so much hinges on the name of the group that all you need to do is give it a bad name and you've blown the whole gig no matter what the music's like.

So it wasn't a conscious attempt at anonymity?

No. Not in the least. No, because we presumed that everyone would know what it was all about. That it would be an open joke.

My mind also went back to the time when Paul wanted The Beatles to go out as Rory and The Redstreaks or some such name when their career was at a peak, so that they could just go out and rock without the drawback of their Beatle history and the expectations that would involve.

Yeh. Well, it's a tempting fantasy, isn't it? If you want to go out and do rock without requests and expectations then you change your name, I suppose. But it really never lasts.

Was there ever any hassle about taking the musicians away from Delaney and Bonnie in order to form The Dominos?

I can't really remember that. I don't think there was. No, not between me and Delaney.

Was Phil Spector involved at all in the 'Layla' album?

What happened was that before we did any gigs or anything and just as The Dominos were hanging out at my house George (Harrison) was going to do 'All Things Must Pass', so he asked if we'd

72

like to play on it because he hadn't really got a band. I think he'd got Klaus and Ringo mainly. So we agreed and we did a lot of that album as just a back-up band. Then I said, 'Well, one day we'd like to do an album too, you know, because we've got a couple of songs ... do you think we could use some of your session time if you're not going to use it, just to put something down?' Phil was in on this and he produced a version of 'Tell The Truth' and 'Roll It Over'. We were going to put it out as a single but no one really wanted it.

So nothing on the album was done by Spector?
No. It was before that.

How would you evaluate Duane Allman's contribution to 'Layla'?
Well, I can tell you that we were in the studio for three days before he showed up and got about two tracks done. Then when he arrived, we sort of hit it off and we did the rest of the album, both records, in less than ten days. I mean the first three days we went in there and we struggled and we put two of the songs on there and then he showed up and that was just it. It just took off. He was the catalyst for the whole thing.

Was he a challenge?
No. I couldn't look at it like that. He was into a different style of playing altogether. He was an inspiration. What would have been a challenge would have been for someone to have come in to play exactly like me, but he played exactly like him.

How did you first meet him?
Well, we were in Criteria Studios, Miami, and he came down with the Allman Brothers to do a gig in a huge park near Miami Beach. So we said let's take the night off and go over and see him because I'd heard him before on record. And I just remember driving down to this park, and while we were parking the car about half a mile from this open-air gig I just heard this wailing guitar coming through the air, louder than anything else. You could just hear the band and then this really high in the air sound like a siren. It was just amazing. We walked down to the gig, sat down in front of the bandstand and there were The Allman Brothers. They were just a sight to behold when they were all together because they all looked like one another for a start. They were all very thin, all with very

long hair floating in the wind, and rocking like you've never fucking heard. Then that night after the gig they came back to the studio and jammed . . . and Duane stopped for the rest of the album.

Another chance meeting?
Yeh.

What sort of studio conditions prevailed throughout the recording of 'Layla' because you were already into H by then, weren't you?
Yeh. Towards the end of the sessions we got a couple of fatherly advice lectures from guys in charge – from Ahmet Ertegun and Tom Dowd. They were just concerned because it was so open. We were just in there with grass and hash and uppers and downers, coke, H, beer, wine . . . everything you could get that would do something to you. T, H, C . . . everything was out there, everyone was doing it. It'll never happen again anything like that. It was so full ahead. Everybody in there was into it and just rocking on. It became like an envelope, a little vacuum, that place did. If you went out on the street you felt like you were in a different world altogether. So it was like a womb.

So nobody was straight for any of the time?
Except for anyone who was producing or engineering.

Heroin stopped you playing for so long. How did it accelerate you on this occasion?
Well, it's something that you can keep up for just so long as a communal thing. Like anything else, it's not the drug; it's just the fact that once you get heavily into something with five or six or seven people, you can only go on at that rate for a certain time before someone gets weak and peels off and then it starts to decay. We all got into H throughout that and then dropped it and went on tour. It was that sort of stopping and starting thing with me – I went on and then off for about three months before starting again.

How did you get on in the first place?
It was in England when we first started 'All Things Must Pass'. I actually was scoring coke and the guy that I was getting it from was saying to me, 'I can't get you any unless you agree to buy some H as well,' which is a certain way they deal. So I said, fine . . . right

74

... and I got a phial of coke and half a phial of H, that was the deal. So I keep stashing this H away in a drawer thinking, fuck, I don't want to know about that, I'll just use the coke. Then one day I thought, well, what's it like this naughty drug? So I tried it and thought, OK ... and it was quite a long stretch before I hit what could be called a 'habit' where I really had to go out and get some more. It could have been up to a year before that really took hold. It was very slow. I think a lot of people that get addicted get addicted right off the bat, but with me it was a take it or leave it thing for quite a long time. Of course, it's a pretty rotten trick because I would probably have never started if it hadn't have been in my house, bought for and just lying around.

Have you ever asked yourself why there's such a strong relationship between musicians and heroin?

It's a rationality. You can only rationalise it. I don't think you can actually say for sure. I think you can rationalise it by saying musicians live on a very intense emotional plane of necessity, and heroin is probably the strongest pain killer you can lay your hands on.

Well, another reasonable suggestion I've heard put forward is that the 'high' a musician gets from performing is so high and yet so momentary that heroin is one of the ways of recapturing it when not on-stage.

Yeh. You're absolutely right and that's a very good point because a musician lives to be high. That's twenty times as addictive as H.

How much did the H used to cost you?

Well, the cost sort of rose until it was double at the end of the time I was taking it. I think it was £150 for a half ounce to begin with and then it went up to £250–300; what you could get through if you had a habit like mine, not using a needle and thinking that I could always afford it, was something like an ounce a week. And so with all the rip-offs taken into consideration, I could be spending sometimes up to £1000 a week.

Is there any particular song of yours which you prize over all the rest?

Yeh, but that's only because it's one of the last I put on record. It's on the new album (at that time '461 Ocean Boulevard'). Actually I'm proud of a couple of them. One's called 'Give Me Strength' and one's called 'Let It Grow'. I am proud of them because they were done very quickly and they sound good on record and they were the last things I achieved. I'm never going to be that proud of stuff I've done in the past. Before this album the only thing that meant anything to me was 'Layla', which was because it was actually about an emotional experience, a woman that I felt really deeply about and that turned me down, and I had to kind of pour it out in some way. So we wrote these songs, made an album, and the whole thing was great.

What did the woman in question think?
She didn't give a damn.

Did you ever think you could say things to her through the album that maybe you couldn't face to face? Did you ever think you'd get through to her that way?
Yeh, I did think that. And also the emotional content of some of the blues on it, you know. But no, man. I mean, her husband is a great musician. It's the wife-of-my-best-friend scene and her husband has been writing great songs for years about her and she still left him. You see, he grabbed one of my chicks and so I thought I'd get even with him one day, on a petty level, and it grew from that. She was trying to attract his attention, trying to make him jealous, and so she used me, you see, and I fell madly in love with her. If you listen to the words of 'Layla': I tried to give you consolation/ When your old man had let you down/Like a fool, I fell in love with you/You turned my whole world upside down.

Do you need to go through a crisis to write?
Yeh, I think I did.

Where did the name Layla come from?
It comes from a Persian love story written in the eleventh or twelfth century, a sort of love story, that's all. It's called *Layla and Mashnoun*.

Does Layla reject Mashnoun then?
No, neither of them rejects the other. It's like boy meets girl but parents don't dig it.

That was nothing to do with your experience, was it?
Not really. It was just that I liked the name and the story was beautifully written. I related to it in that way.

76

Did you consciously write 'Layla' as a concept album about un-requited love?

Well, it was the heaviest thing going on at the time so, yeh, I suppose it came about like that. I didn't consciously do it, though, it just happened that way. That was what I wanted to write about most of all.

How long did it take to write all the songs on 'Layla'?

The band had been together living at the house for about three or four months and so songs were semi-written, or at least certain songs were semi-written, before we got into the studio. I mean . . . inasmuch as we'd spend all night playing 'Johnny B. Goode' for four hours so it was like whenever we did get an idea. It was a very communal idea.

But the songs that are yours must have been written on acoustic guitar first.

As far as I can remember I wrote them on my own and then had to introduce them to the band in the studio, because when we were at home we would never seriously sit down and say 'Well now, we'll run through this song or that song.' They were just like jams. We'd jam but we'd get very together on everything, so that I knew that if I did write a song I could just produce it and they'd get into it straight away.

And that's how you got into 'Layla'?

Yeh, most of them. I think so.

Rehearsed at home?

No, I don't think I ever played them to them at home. It was just that when it was time to cut the album we went to Miami, and then I said 'This is what I've got', and they picked it up quickly.

So when were the songs actually written?

I would say that seventy-five per cent of each song was written in that period while we were rehearsing at home and the rest was contributed to in the studio.

Can you actually remember writing 'Layla'?

Now that was a very, very combined effort really. I remember writing the words and the changes but the things that make the song what it is – like the riff and the end part – were done in the studio and that was an inspiration from using Duane. Actually you can tell when Duane arrives in the studio because the album is done chronologically. The numbers are placed in the order they were recorded.

'I looked Away' first and so on?

Yeh . . . and you can tell when Duane arrives because then every thing picks up a little bit and goes a step higher.

You wrote 'Layla' as a set of lyrics at first?

Yeh . . . over changes but nothing spectacular. It was nothing you'd think twice about if you heard it. It was only after Duane arrived and I'd said 'Would you mind playing on the album?' that we sat down and composed the lines and things. There are so many parts on that track, it's unbelievable.

Did you feel you'd actually achieved something when you'd got it down?

You're fucking right. (laughs). Too fucking right.

How long did it take to record?

It wasn't long . . . (Enter Albhy Galutin, Miami session musician who has played on 'Layla', '461 Ocean Boulevard' and 'One In Every Crowd'). Do you want to take part in this interview, Albhy? You were there at the time. You remember. You must remember as well as I do.

Albhy: You played everything during the whole two weeks. What kept it so magic was that instead of saying we're going to cut this song today, you would just play all the songs all of the time as they were developed.

That's right, yeh. We were doing things like playing back all the songs that were cut and just adding to them bit by bit and taking things out or . . .

Albhy: Actually I wasn't there when you cut 'Layla', but although you didn't do it until right near the end it'd already been played on for at least five different days in some form or another.

78

Was the original idea to have a theme running through the album?

No, the idea wasn't even to have a double album. It was the thing where you've got so many tracks that you can't decide what to use, so you decide that if you cut two or three more maybe you can make a double album. It was like we weren't into making decisions about anything so we just let it flow. We carried on and we got a double album and there are probably still tracks left over that we didn't use.

They're all very much 'Baby's gone and left me' songs.

That was all very subconscious. That was just the way it happened. We didn't sit down and think about it.

Even the songs that weren't yours such as 'Have You Ever Loved A Woman' help to sustain the theme.

Yeh . . . well, they just seemed appropriate at the time. That's all.

You couldn't have done better if you'd have tried to make a concept album about unrequited love.

Yeh. Now I'm trying to make an album about requited love and it's harder still. How do you make an album about requited love? I'm trying now but the songs I've written are very boring.

What do you mean by boring?

Well, they're very sort of middle of the road. I was telling Albhy the other day. I was playing him the songs I've written with George Terry and they're very – all honeysuckle and blossoms, sweetness and light, a bit . . . ughhhh . . . if you know what I mean.

Do you think, therefore, that if you're reasonably content your work loses some of that vicious edge?

Well, of course, it follows somehow doesn't it. How can you be vicious if you're content? You can't be viciously content.

Where did you meet Tom Dowd?

It goes back to when Cream first came to America. I can't remember how but somehow or other we got into Atlantic studios – I think we wanted to put some tracks down and someone said, 'Hire Atlantic Studios because that's the best' – and he was the engineer. I mean, can you believe that! A band comes into town and Tommy Dowd is the fucking engineer. No, do you know what we were actually

79

doing? We were using Atlantic Studios to rehearse in for playing the Murray the K Show and Tom Dowd was just wandering around. Felix Pappalardi came in one day and said 'That's a fucking hit group. Let's cut something,' so we just played a few numbers and Tom was on the case. I don't know what he was doing or why he should've been there.

What did those cuts eventually become?

That became 'Disraeli Gears'. Tom cut 'Disraeli Gears'.

Albhy: There's only two records on Tommy's wall even though he's got hundreds and hundreds of gold records. The only two on his wall are 'Good Lovin' by The Rascals because he told them to cut it, they didn't want to do it, and 'Sunshine Of Your Love'. I remember he talked to me about it and I think it was his drumbeat and he was very proud of it.

You really work well together?

He's the king. He's the king. Musically I respect him probably more than any other musician in the world and he's not even a musician. He just knows what's right and what's wrong. He tells me when to stop and when to start and I take that as the law.

When you'd completed 'Layla' did you think you'd just recorded your best work ever?

Yes and no. I don't know . . . it's hard to remember.

Albhy: I seem to remember everybody feeling that it was obvious something very special had just happened.

Did it sell well?

It didn't sell a fucking copy for about two years. Now it sells more each year than it has the previous year. It didn't even make the charts in Britain although the single got in about three years after the album came out. You see, I just refused to have my name displayed across the album.

Do you think that was a contributing factor?

I don't know. Perhaps if I had it would never have become a hit. Perhaps they like Derek and The Dominos better than Eric Clapton. You see now you're talking about England. In America music tends to sell on it's own merit. You can turn on the radio there and hear a record by a group you've never even heard of, and it's just got straight in the charts.

And yet now 'Layla' is rated as a 'rock classic'.

Yes, it is. About bloody time too! (laughs).

Why did you refuse to display your name on the album?

Because it started out as Derek and The Dominos and I figured it should go out as that. It was a share and share alike group. Everyone played an equal part and I didn't want any advantage over people who weren't that well known. So, the pay was always equal and we did a tour of England playing the filthiest clubs we could find just so that I could get back down with people again.

So it was a reaction against being set up as an individual?

Yes, of course. I just wanted to get back to a level that would make me feel at home. Just to join in all the vomiting and horribleness.

What hadn't felt like home?

Being alone. Being a soloist rather than a member of a group. I'd rather be a member of a group than a virtuoso. I'm going around now doing tours and shows as 'Eric Clapton and his Band' and it feels like I'm 'out there' a bit too much . . . like Clapton *and his Band*. They're really twice as good as I am. Any one of them can rock me out. I can flake out and they're still going on. It's not a humility trip. I'm not fucking humble. I just like to be in a position where I can shout and not feel that I'm shouting louder than anyone else. I'd like to be just equal, not humble.

Were you pleased with the live Dominos album?

I don't think I've listened to it much actually. You can remind me about it if you like . . . Side One, track one?

'Why Does Love Got To Be So Sad'. That seems to fit in with the feel of 'Layla'.

Yeh. It was written in that period before we went to Miami. I don't think I had much control over that album coming out. I must admit I don't particularly like live albums – they're not my forte. I tend to go on stage with the attitude 'Oh it's only a one-night stand. We'll only be here one night.' Carl Radle is a very bad influence on me that way. He just comes wandering around the dressing room saying 'Whatever's gonna be is gonna be' and 'It's all right' and 'It's all gonna work out all right', so I can go on stage thinking 'Fuck . . . I'm only going to be here one night. I can do whatever I like and get out quick before they catch me.' So I tend to do sort of spontaneous idiotic things which really aren't very good when you listen to them back. It's a spontaneous event and everyone's taking part and that's it. They don't look good under glass.

Do you feel that about the Rainbow Concert?
Yeh. Absolutely.

Live Cream?
Yeh . . . especially. I think we sounded as though we were playing through transistors but at a very loud volume.

Were there plans for a second Dominos album in the studios?
Yeh, but that's when we broke up see because we'd done 'Layla', and we were especially pleased with that and we came back to England and we tried to recreate that whole situation in an English studio – Olympic. Tommy Dowd wasn't there and we had no one in control. We had Andy Johns engineering and we were trying to produce ourselves, I think.

You had all the songs together then?
I had the songs and we did the tracks but then half-way through arguments were starting for no reason. People would just start having rows with one another and it would just get to the point where someone would say, 'Well, I'm going home. Why don't you call in that session drummer or why don't you call in that piano player. . . . ?' And I'd just say, 'Well all right. I'm fucking off,' and I'd go home and leave them all there. I just lost my temper so many times that I thought 'That's it. The fucking group has ended.'

Why did that come about?
We were all just trying to recreate the situation we'd got into while recording 'Layla'. It was such a peak for all of us. It was a one-off situation . . . unique . . . and we just all tried to get in there and do the same thing again and we just blew our minds. The fuses went completely. We could maybe have done it if we'd gone back to

Miami and hung out with the same people and had Tom producing and all the other stuff that was going on.

Albhy: Duane was awful important. Anything he was ever on was like someone had turned up the voltage.

Yeh, he could turn me on and off like a light. It was just like if he came in the room you'd stand up.

Albhy: I've seen him come into sessions late off a plane, and he'd come in with his guitar strapped on with the chord in his hands looking for an amp. You could get three more takes off any song with him there than you ever could without him.

So you actually broke up in the studios then?

Yeh. Half-way through several takes. But it was time. It wasn't going to go much further. It really wasn't. I think it was on it's last legs. We'd done that 'Layla' album and then we'd gone on the road and really ploughed ourselves into the ground. There was a long long tour where we played all those shitty towns like South Bend Indiana and all that. And, of course, that was also the beginning of when I hit smack or when smack hit me – one of the two. When I got smacked.

And that contributed to the break up?

Oh yeh, because 'Layla' was done during the period when we were dabbling and fucking around with everything. It was like a snort of coke in one nostril, a snort of smack in the other, a pint of cheap wine in one ear, a bottle of Scotch in the other – it was just full out. It worked for that period. 'Layla' survived that and was actually good because of it, and then the tour went on and we started to get further and further apart into our own little cabinets. It just ended up fighting and after that I didn't do anything.

That was the start of the layoff?

Yeh. I went back home and stayed there and locked all the doors.

Had you been disappointed with the response to 'Layla'?

Yeh. Having done it and thinking it was the best thing I'd done to have nobody bother to go and listen to it was a bit of a drag. There are a certain amount of people that you would like to hear an album. I mean, if you've got an album that you're really proud of, there are certain people that you would like to be turned on by it.

83

Apple Records run a thing whereby they send out all their new releases to their friends or to other musicians and those are probably the people that you always want to please first. I didn't have that sort of thing going. I wasn't sending out free albums and so I was disappointed that people that I respected in the music world didn't really hear it for a while. They didn't even hear about it. I mean the Promo office went through a thing about doing 'Eric is Derek' badges just so that people might have a clue to the fact that the album was really me.

So they thought this was one of the reasons why the album hadn't taken off?

Yeh. They tried to get me to put my name on the album cover in England, but in America I was allowed to have the cover just as the painting – no words on it, no logo, nothing – just the painting. In England the Polydor Marketing Board wouldn't have it.

Do you have any control over your album art-work?

Fuck all. I finally chose the cover for 'One In Every Crowd' after really wrangling because there's this Marketing Board that's set up now. The cover was originally going to be that insert drawing of a guy and they said, 'No. It's too much like "Planet Waves". It won't go out. We're not having it.' So I had to sit and leaf through these things that they thought were album covers until I finally put one together myself that had my name on it and that appealed to them. It was my idea, it was just that they'd forced me to do something which they'd agree to.

The Lean Years
In Hibernation, 1971–4

Did you have ideas of forming bands during the layoff period?

No. I can't say that I did. I felt very much of a solo artist during that time. It wasn't my ambition at that particular time to go out and do anything but just lay around.

So how did you spend a typical day?

Nothing. Watched TV, built models . . . . It's funny, when I got to the end of that hibernation I thought, well fuck, look at the time I've wasted. I haven't really done anything with my life. Then suddenly I discovered this great hoard of cassettes which I'd forgotten all about but which I'd been doing all the time. Not many of them were actually usable songs but a lot of them were incredible performances. It's like I'd sit down and play a blues with just a guitar and when I played it back I thought, who the fuck is that? Sounds good! So I was blaming myself for not keeping my hand in when in actual fact I was still playing and singing as much as any other time.

Did you get bored?

You don't get bored on smack. That's something you do not get!

You once went to Paris with The Who?

Yeh, but that was just for a day. I could take enough to survive for a day and then get back by nightfall to score some more.

Did Pete Townshend take you to see that gig to get you in the mood for the Rainbow gig?

I don't know. I don't know his motivation for anything really. He's a very mysterious person to me is Pete and I just don't completely understand him. I think he's great and I admire him, but I would never try and do a thesis on him. That's beyond me. I just don't know why he picked on me to do the Rainbow Concert. It could've been anybody but I'm grateful he chose me. I was just pleased to be doing it because I wouldn't have made up my mind to do it on my own. It had to be someone dragging me around by the scruff of my collar and making me do this and that.

Yet strangely enough it went against the grain of what you were trying to do with The Dominos by pushing you to the fore.

Yeh, well maybe I needed it. I don't know.

How did you feel about the gig?

I thought it was OK. I had a good time doing it. It was when I listened to the tapes afterwards that I realised that it was well under par. It was like a charity benefit in a way, you know. They got me out, got me on stage and tried to get me at it and I was being pushed more than I was pulling. I did it really because it was for Pete (Townshend) most of all. I wasn't really ready to go on stage. Although my reluctance was great I really loved the feeling. The welcome I got really moved me, it really did.

What specific musical criticisms did you have?

It's hard to remember now. I think the music was reasonably OK, I just think there were too many people on-stage for the way it was recorded. They recorded it on something like an eight-track and so they had to mix a lot of things together while they were recording, which meant that the rhythm section suffered and you got the bass and drums mixed in together. It was just not very satisfactory in that aspect. I mean, it was very hard to mix.

So you weren't disappointed with your licks?

Well, I mean, I didn't think they were great. They were reasonable. Everyone made mistakes and what I heard when I heard the tapes back was how many mistakes we all made. But then I'm very self-critical in that way.

Who got you to the Bangla Desh concert?

George. It really was an expedition. I got there a week in advance because they called for rehearsals to be a week in advance – 'The gig is on Saturday, please be there on Monday', sort of thing. So I arranged by long-distance phone calls that there'd be something there for me because the habit was going strong. So I fly over and there's nothing there and we can't score. There was no way we could score because the only thing people seem to take in New York is smack cut by ninety-five per cent, nothing or talcum powder, and so they have to shoot it up in order to get any kind of buzz. I wasn't into that. I didn't really want to go that far and so it was just a question of lying on this hotel bed going through agony with people going out trying to get stronger and stronger stuff each time. All of it was just like talcum powder. So finally one of the cameramen came up with this medicine that he took for his ulcers which turned out to be a heroin substitute – Methadone. It got me straight enough so that I could go on stage and play. It was like the last day and on the day of the gig these guys got me the right thing to get me standing on-stage, not looking too green, managing to know which way the audience was looking. I just managed it by the skin of my teeth otherwise I'd never have got off the bed.

You heard playbacks of the tapes presumably?

Yeh. I think they're fucking awful. I think I played so badly.

Albhy: I tell you, I was at that concert and hadn't seen you since 'Layla' and, man, it almost broke my heart.

Yeh, it wasn't me at all. I just wasn't there. I wasn't there at all.

Had you ever considered how 'the layoff' has become a part of the archetypal rock career? Dylan's neck break ... The Beatles and Maharishi. ...

It's probably necessary because, when you work, you work so fucking hard. It's physical and mental. It's so hard. It's not like a job where you can just stand there all day and stick bricks on top of one another and think about something else while you're doing it. It's concentration and mental fatigue and if you do it long enough you just run yourself into the fucking ground. You've got to have a break and that break can last forever sometimes.

Is it also because people's expectations get harder and harder to satisfy? You want to be a musician and the public wants a myth?

No ... no, I don't think so. It's always a conversation between you and yourself. Other people don't come into it. It's always your own expectations that are the hardest to live up to and other people just don't have any influence upon that whatsoever. You know what you can do, what you've done and what you might be able to do and that's what you have to live up to all of the time. It's not what other people say because at a certain stage in your life you decide that comments from other directions just aren't going to make any difference. It's your own thing that you've got to live with. That's what'll run you into the ground if you try to force it.

How was it that you heard about the acupuncture treatment?

I think that my girl-friend's dad was pretty concerned about her and his concern reached me. He'd heard about Meg the acupuncturist and said wouldn't it be worth a try. I said, 'Fuck off ... no!! Where's me dope!' It finally came down to the point where I could see that he was worried about her so I thought, well, OK if it gets her off, I don't mind going along with it because I can see the concern of a father for his daughter and I'm not doing any good, so let her see if she can get cured. I wasn't actually looking for a cure myself. I was quite happy to go on. It just so happened that I got cured as well.

How did the cure start?

We tried for a week to do it at home but it was just impossible because we had hidden stashes everywhere. We'd suddenly be half-way through a treatment and think 'Oh, I know where there's some' – like Winnie the Pooh forgetting where he'd stashed his pot of honey.

Did you know what the treatment actually involved when you started or did you think it involved traditional acupuncture rather than electro-acupuncture?

I didn't really care. Yeh, I did think it would be long needles stuck down the back of my head or somewhere like that – something particularly unpleasant. It was pretty unpleasant as a matter of fact. That voltage thing is very strange because you have this machine with little metal clips that you clip on each earlobe, and then you have an electric current running through them from one side to another, you see, so it passes straight through your skull. The instruction is that you turn up the voltage control, the volume of voltage, until it's painful and then sit there and bear it for an hour or two. That is a drag. I mean, you sit there with your finger in an electric socket for a couple of hours and see if you really dig it.

And yet you used to go to sleep like that?
No.

I've seen you asleep with it on.

Really, with the machine on? I must have built up some tolerance against the electricity then.

Does the treatment take away the craving?

I hate that word craving. No, of course it doesn't. That's what I've always said to Meg. 'Have you lost the desire?' – I'd say, 'What are you talking about? If I lost my desire I'd be a walking shell. Desire covers a big field.'

How do you think it cures then?

I think it was just isolation. Something in the fact that it was an electric current running through my head made me stop wanting to take smack. I don't know. But it certainly hasn't made me stop wanting to play the guitar or wanting something or other.

No, I'm not talking about losing all your human desires. I'm meaning that once you were on smack and having started you were compelled to keep it up – there was no breaking it. Yet when you began this treatment you were able to lose that compulsion and break it.

Yeh. Well, I mean, it was so painful that it couldn't have been worse than actually coming down. The psychology behind it is like Albhy right now is itching his head. Now, if it really itches bad, the best thing for him to do would be to pinch himself in the leg so bad hard that it hurts more than the itch on his head, you see.

Albhy: Did you have physical withdrawal?
No.

Albhy: Did it stop that?
Yeh. I had one day of having cramps and the rest of the time was OK. That's what I think it does. It's just more of a sensation than the one you'd be experiencing if you weren't using it.

That period of treatment certainly changed you though. You were really down at one point telling me that all you could see was the waste of the past, the pain of the present and the darkness of the future. You were almost going to sell your guitars, weren't you?

Yeh. I told one of the roadies to sell them for whatever price he could get and score. It was down to selling house and cars. I couldn't get cash from anywhere.

Facing the Image

Do you ever consider how other people see you, in terms of image?

I try as best as I can to control it by throwing them into confusion as much as I can. Does that answer your question?

Partly. How do you think people see you at this point, though? You must know that, because you have to know in order to throw people into confusion.

No, I don't really know how anyone thinks of me and I don't really know how to throw them into confusion. It's always been a guess. Someone will give away something by making a comment about what I seem to be so I think, 'Well, fuck you – I'll show you another side of me that you've never even suspected.'

What's an example of that?

Well, people seemed to think that I was a very studious religious young man whereas in actual fact they hadn't seen the wilder side, so I'd throw that part of me around for a bit. I don't mean to say by that that I don't enjoy being a lunatic, I mean I love it. I'll carry on being like that for the rest of my life but I have other sides as well. It's just that if people decide they're going to settle down with any one side, they'd better watch out for the other!

How did the lunatic element develop – as displayed on your last US tour?

It's always been there. It's nothing new. I mean, right from school I was more or less 'sent to Coventry' all my life because me and a couple of other guys would be the loonies of the school. We'd be into making faces or inventing strange creatures that we'd portray while other kids were playing cricket and football. We were always looked on as being a bit weird so that side of my character has always been lurking in the background just ready to find a soul mate. All I need is someone like Larry Smith or Keith to go off with and I'm happy as a sand boy.

What about that time you streaked while in flight?

Oh, on a commercial airline . . . yeh. But, I mean, it's been worse on charter flights where you've had three or four people peeling off. Oh dear . . . that gets very strange.

I would have thought it was more outrageous on a commercial flight.

Of course, of course. But I really don't think I'm that dynamic. I wasn't trying to impress anybody. No way. I just remember when streaking came in I probably always wanted to be on the avante garde of that and so I was a sort of late in life streaker. I mean, I did it on the beach a couple of places too. Sometimes I was drunk, other times just slightly drunk and semi-provoked by a bourgeois situation or something. On the commercial flight they really panicked. I never got over that. They've never left me and they watch me like a fucking hawk now. Sometimes you can get a flight from London to Jamaica and you stop off in somewhere but they won't let me off the plane. They let everyone off the plane but me.

Didn't you turn up late at the opening of 'Manhattan Follies' and then start blowing on a duck caller?

Yeh, I was asked to leave from that as well. It was one of Robert's (Stigwood) productions and so I felt quite safe in doing it. I turned up late and a bit over the hill with my duck whistle. It was a joke show . . . you would've loved it. They asked me to leave very politely.

Was Robert embarrassed that you had to be asked to leave?

No. I could see him at another table saying to someone, 'Get him out of here for fuck's sake.' It was his idea!

Why do you constantly change your appearance?

It doesn't seem to make sense. A lot of people reach a look which they like – like someone who has a short back and sides and shaves every morning. You get into that routine of going to the barber once a week for your trim. Well, that kind of life isn't possible for me. I can't live that way in any other respect so I can't do it with my appearance either because I'm all over the place. I might be here, I might be somewhere else, and I just have to adapt to the surroundings. I suppose that if I was at home with a regular little job and a routine of some kind I'd look like what I was supposed to be . . . if that makes sense!

Are you always dissatisfied?

No. I don't really notice it because I don't look in the mirror a lot. I suppose I used to at one time but I don't now, so that when I do I think how could I have been going around like that and I want to do something about it. Also, it's getting ridiculous now because people are always making comments about it. They say, 'Oh, you're always changing your appearance.' They say, 'Oh, you've got a beard now,' and I don't know how to react – whether I should have a beard or what I should be looking like.

At other times you've obviously taken on the look of the period. For instance, the perm.

I did that as an out and out tribute to Jimi. I thought that if I had hair like his I'd probably be able to play like that as well. Really. A sign of immaturity I think. I think I've grown up now.

Were you ever into being a mod?

When I was a young man, yes. Why not!

You were very fashion conscious?

Well, not fashion conscious as much as dress conscious. In fact I thought fashion was fucking awful and I still think it is.

So how did you counter it?

I just avoided it like the plague. Followed my nose, I suppose.

But then you started the military jacket craze.

Yeh. But then I don't know where that kind of thing comes from. I suppose it's just that I've always loved well-made clothes. I always liked to get old clothes that were well-made rather than something that looks good but falls apart. You see, I got into a thing when I was about seventeen or eighteen of American clothes because they were being made really well – all these amazing fabrics like Dacron. So I got into an Ivy League thing with three buttons, a crewcut and white socks and loved all that for a bit.

There must have come a point where you began to notice that what you were wearing was cropping up in the audience?

Well, that was just the little legend thing going on, wasn't it? The following say with The Yardbirds was a little pack that followed us around and would pick up on what to wear on the occasion of the gig, what to be seen in the audience with. Which is fashion, isn't it?

I find it amusing that while the kids were copying you, you were copying someone else. Like with the perm and Hendrix. You were as easily influenced as they were.

Yeh. I was really quite dogmatic in my early twenties about what to wear. I was really on about it. But later, and now for instance, I don't give a fuck. I think I've lost the drive for that. If I did have the drive I'd be out and about seeing the shops and seeing what I'd like to wear.

You had some pretty fancy stuff made up for you in the Cream days.

Yeh. We were pretty smart dressers in those days.

How did you feel about being voted one of the rock world's next fatalities?

I thought great, you know! They're never going to get me (laughs). I don't care what they say. I mean, they like to create that kind of mystique I know. They want to get a lot of people there to see if so-and-so's going to die on-stage. I mean, think what an event that'd be! But it's all a joke. I'm sure they don't really mean it. You see, Keith (Richard) was top of the list and what would they do if Keith died? They'd feel pretty sorry about putting that in their paper for a start (laughs). It's vicarious . . . they want to see someone else do it, see if they can get their rocks off that way. Well, I'm a bit like that myself – not to the extent that I'd want to see someone die on-stage – but I remember I used to go to Ronnie Scott's Club when Phil Seamen was the house drummer and he would literally come out of the dressing room and crawl across the floor because that's the only kind of energy he had. And then he'd get behind the kit and it was magic! I'm impressed by that kind of thing, very definitely.

Presence of the Lord

I heard that you had a 'Spiritual revelation' when you were in the States one time?

Two guys came to my dressing room. They were just two Christians and they said, 'Can we pray with you?' I mean, what can you do? So we knelt down and prayed and it was really like the blinding light and I said, 'What's happening, I feel much better!' And then I said to them, 'Let me show you this poster I've got of Jimi Hendrix.' I pulled it out and there was a portrait of Christ inside which I hadn't bought, had never seen in my life before. And it just knocked the three of us sideways. From then on I became a devout Christian until this situation occurred, the three . . . the triangle.

How did that knock you out?

It just knocked me out that . . . I'm going to mention names. It was George, right? And the fact that he'd been into Transcendental Meditation for so long and yet couldn't keep his wife . . . I mean, his wife just didn't want to know. All she wanted was for him to say 'I love you,' and all he was doing was meditating. That shook my faith completely. I still pray and I still see God in other people more than I see Him in the sky or anything like that.

In 1970 you were quoted as saying you now wanted to write songs about Jesus.

That was probably when I moved down here. That's when I wrote 'Presence Of The Lord'. You see, I was on the run for a start. Pilcher (a well-known London policeman) was after me. He wanted me because he was a groupie cop. He got George and he got John and Mick and the rest of them. So I was on the run from flat to flat and when I finally got out of town the pressure was off. It was such a relief, man, and it was just such a beautiful place that I sat down and wrote the song.

So you were superimposing your religious experience on to the actual situation of being on the run? Rather like the early Negro spirituals?

Exactly. At the time you couldn't separate the two things. It was the first song I ever wrote.

Could you clarify your religious stance?

I wish I could. I'll definitely try. Let's say that I believe in a god and that god I suppose is everybody's god. It's not my god or some-one else's god that I'd like to know. I think He's everybody's god and I like sharing Him. But I can't chain myself down to any one material aspect of Him over another. Like I can't say that I believe in the Bible any more than I do in a television set because one can inform me about god just as much as the other inasmuch as every-thing, everything you come into contact with is a result of His work. Therefore you can see as much of Him in anything as in anything else.

So you don't believe in any concept of salvation?

You mean resurrection or . . . ?

No, that man is damned without a salvation from God.

No, I can't believe that . . . no. I suppose I've got really a very lax view in that I think that God is still as much in control as He ever was in that whatever's going on is His will.

Fatalistic?

Sort of.

So you believe the outcome is going to be the same whatever a person believes or does. . . . There's no need for man to make a choice?

No, there's no need for man to make a choice because he has to make a choice. There's no need for a need because from the word go, from birth, a man is placed between two different factions. He has to make a choice. He can't help it. That's God's work too. So there's no reason to make a choice because from what you know to be right and wrong in your heart you'll make that choice. Thinking about it and considering it seemingly has nothing to do with it. It gets back to what I've said before that your heart should rule your head in terms of belief, because when you start to analyse any feeling you have about a spiritual thing you stop feeling it. You haven't got time to feel it any more. You haven't got time for both.

It depends on whether you believe there are any absolute values that stand outside you, doesn't it . . . by which your heart could be wrong?

Well . . . if you've got an example of that. . . .

95

Well, would you have told Charles Manson to follow his heart?

I wouldn't try and tell him anything else. I can't imagine what I'd tell him if I thought I could actually have an effect on him. Ultimately a man's choice about what he's doing is his own.

You think a man is responsible before God for his choices?

Of course, yeh.

Will he be judged on those choices?

I don't know.

This is where a television isn't going to tell you much.

That's where a television isn't going to tell you much? You see, I don't know if you're not judged as you actually perform any kind of act. That has rubbed off on me from the Hindu religion in that it seems to make sense. I mean it's a very scientific view – action and reaction. It's like saying the minute you do something evil you let in room for evil, so you are judged in a way.

How did you develop this interest in religious subject matter?

It's a very attractive thing. It's the most intangible thing that you can think of when you get down to it. You can estimate an answer to everything else because there's so little fear, but when it comes to God there are so many people shoving fire and damnation down your throat that it's a very fascinating subject. You feel you should believe in something you know.

I suppose any study of the blues necessarily leads you into gospel, and then you've worked with Leon Russell and Delaney Bramlett, who again have this 'religious flavour' about them. Then with your relationship with George Harrison and your one-time encounter with Christians did you feel that religion was pursuing you in a way?

Could be. Maybe that's it. I really can't put my finger on it because I only know that when I come into touch with someone who's very deeply into a religious thing I shy away. I tend to think, well, I can't see how he's into it that deep or how he's performed this ritual because it always does at some point demand a ritual or a routine of some kind which somehow doesn't make sense to me. From an outside point of view it sometimes doesn't tie in with the belief, it actually contradicts the belief at many points. I can't be specific but

96

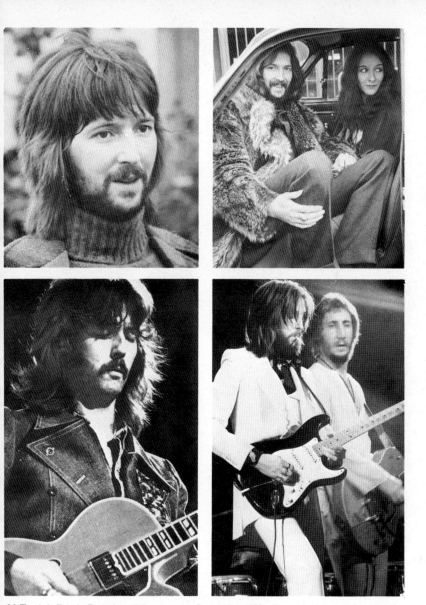

36 *Top left:* Eric in Paris for a Who concert, September 1972—'I could take enough to survive for a day and then get back by nightfall to score some more' 37 *Top right:* With Alice Ormsby-Gore 38 *Above left:* At the concert for Bangla Desh, Madison Square Garden, New York, August 1971—'It wasn't me at all. I just wasn't there' 39 *Above right:* The Rainbow concert, January 1973. Eric with Pete Townshend—'I wasn't really ready to go on stage'

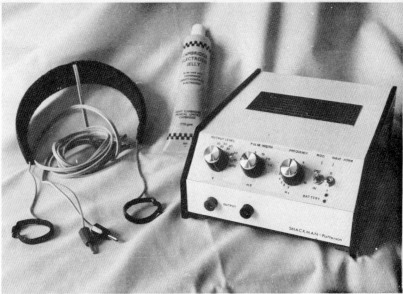

40 *Top:* Dr Meg Patterson with husband George, the electro-acupuncturist who got Eric off heroin 41 *Above:* Equipment for neuro-electric therapy—'You have this machine with little metal clips that you clip on each ear lobe'

42 *Left:* 10 April 1974, Eric and his manager, Robert Stigwood, arrive for his come-back party

43 *Left:* Eric with Pattie Harrison 1975

44 *Above:* On-stage at the Nassau Coliseum, New York

45 *Above:* On the road again

46 *Above:* On-stage in the US 1975

47 *Above:* Eric as The Preacher in 'Tommy'

48 *Above:* During filming of Ken Russell's 'Tommy' *left to right:* John Entwistle, Eric and Pete Townshend

49 *Right:* Eric as loony—'That side of my character has always been lurking in the background...'
50 *Below:* '.. just looking for a soul mate. All I need is someone like Larry Smith...and I'm happy as a sand boy'

51 *Left:* Eric with the author, Steve Turner, Paradise Island, May 1975
52 *Below:* Eric Clapton and his Band 1975

53 Eric, July 1975

there are a lot of religions, especially Eastern ones, where their way of treating people is actually sort of a violation to the belief itself.

This is where I would agree with you. This is where I think you separate truth from non-truth, because for some religions it's not possible for them to be consistent with themselves because they don't match up to the world as it is.

No. That seems to make sense because the minute you form a tradition around everything and decide that that's going to stay the same you've shut out the influence of what's happening in the world or of what's happening anywhere. You're trying to preserve something and nothing is preservable. That's an illusion.

When did you start getting lots of mail from Christians?

It was when I was in Blind Faith at the point when I did 'Presence Of The Lord'. I also had a fairly powerful experience with a couple of Christians during our first tour of the States as I've explained. Probably on that occasion I said that I was interested in what they were doing and so they must have written and told their friends to send me lots of stuff. I think they must have thought that I'd committed myself in a way after that and then I started getting letters. After this, when I failed to come up with the goods, as it were, because I'd got very lax, I started getting very very poisonous letters from them saying, 'What the fuck do you think you're doing? We're sitting around waiting for you to start performing bloody miracles' . . . really, that strong! I thought, well, bugger you! Go and do your own!

Did you ever get any loving humble mail?

Unfortunately most of them were from groups rather than from individuals and they wanted to pester me into doing something, but I do actually get letters from Christian individuals that don't ask for anything. They just say 'Thank you', or say it's nice that you're still doing something or that you helped me . . . I still get some of those. They're good.

What was your experience with Scott Ross, the Jesus Rock DJ?

Well, he ran into me at just about the wrong time. He couldn't have coincided with me at a worse time because I was just getting into smack at the end of The Dominos tour in America. He showed up, we'd met before, and he came around with me. He was trying to get through to me. He did a couple of times. I remember once I scored something like half an ounce and I had a couple of snorts and was going off feeling quite good, and he came around and gave me a big rap about the devil and what have you and I threw the bloody lot down the toilet. I was cursing him for days after that. I wasn't about to turn back ... I was definitely headed on that course and I think I knew it. I knew I was going to see it through. Then there came one night where the guy blew it by saying, 'Come on, I want to pray over you.' I was in a room with three or four other people ... a couple of chicks. He said 'Come on, let's get down on our knees in a circle and I'll do a sermon and we'll all pray together.' Of course, the chicks didn't know who he was ... it was just a freaky thing to say in the middle of a hotel room off the bat, you know.

So I said, 'Well, maybe not *right* now,' because we were getting loose and he just finally exploded. He obviously lost his patience with me and he said, 'Look, I've come to every gig of yours and I've watched you doing your gig – what about you watching me doing mine?' I just thought, 'NO, THAT CAN'T BE IT. Do you mean to say that was the whole thing – he just wanted to do his gig and for us to see it?' I don't think it was as simple as that but that was the way it came out of his mouth because he was at the end of his tether, really up against it. He said things like, 'The Devil's in here and I can't fight him on my own.' It really was quite a put down because someone that heavily into it can tread on someone without even thinking of it – about it – I mean he really did squash me for a second.

You mean what he said wasn't tempered with love?

No. Not at all. It wasn't sympathetic. I went through bad things like a bad trip of thinking I was possessed because he'd said that.

It surprises me to hear you say that you rejected Christianity on the basis that someone into Transcendental Meditation couldn't hold his marriage together.

Well, it was the cause of the break-up between him and his wife. Let's put it that way. It caused him to treat her bad. Although it wasn't Christianity, I can see Christianity in the same situation doing the same thing. It doesn't matter about the fucking religion

98

it just depends on how you interpret and use it. The thing is, say, looking at me and the way I live, for instance, I would find it very hard now to pick up the Bible and read it without having to skip or miss out bits that pointed in my direction because I lead a very very sinful life on the surface of it. I mean, the last time I read the Bible I just thought, well fuck, that's me again He's talking about. And like it kept saying Hell and damnation and that's where I'm going to end up, and I can't believe that I've actually got to stop living the way I do completely or I'll go to Hell. I just don't know how I can equate it to me.

You're basically wanting something that would demand nothing in terms of change?

Probably, yeh.

You're not saying it's not true, you're saying if it's true I don't like it.

(Laughs.) Yeh, probably. I don't know.

If something's true I would have thought it would demand change. If God represents absolute justice then He's certainly . . . I mean, that's why Christ died.

Well, I'm certainly in trouble then, aren't I?

Why?

Well, if the Bible is the truth then what about me? I'm . . . I've committed adultery. . . .

That's wrong.

I'm wrong. Then I drink.

I don't think it says you can't drink.

Oh, it does . . . somewhere. I covet. I haven't murdered anybody yet but I've done just about everything else. I have wealth. . . .

That's not wrong in itself.

Yes, it is. It says in the Bible that it's easier for a camel to pass through the eye of a needle than for a rich man to enter heaven.

Easier. Well, it is. You're pointing that out, aren't you? It's easier but it's not forbidden. I think if you've got more money, then it ties you down a bit. It would obviously make it difficult for you. This is what you're saying now. But it's not a commandment that you

99

shouldn't have money. It's that you have a God that has standards. It's not that you can't have a relationship with Him unless you keep all the commandments because He knows that no one can, but Christ died as a substitute for the punishment you deserve. But it does involve a response from you. It's not like, well, it's there whether you want it or not. You're going to Heaven whether you like it or not . . . sort of thing. It does involve choice on the part of the human because we have choice. St Paul says that the law is a schoolmaster to bring us to the Lord. This is what you're saying – you read it and you find, gosh, I don't fit . . . as I am.

I don't really see that situation changing unless something drastic happens.

Lack of willpower.

No, not so much that as a feeling that I'm right to be where I am. Not right . . . but that I've been placed in this position for a reason. Perhaps it's because I'm being lined up for a humbling experience but you're generally placed somewhere for a purpose, aren't you?

By whom?

By God I should imagine.

But you're waiting for God to turn you into a Christian.

Maybe (laughs). You go to the other extreme. You take everything I say much too far.

I think I see what you mean, but I think you're being much more honest about it because you're saying that the commitment it would involve is frightening rather than saying all religions are basically the same. It seems more like that you're looking for a religion that'll take you and not demand any change at all.

100

Help Me Make It Through Today
Eric Clapton and his Band, 1974–

Getting back to work wasn't a financially-motivated move, was it?
Stopping H pretty much was. I didn't really want to.

It's just that one review I saw aimed a barb at you because during the
Rolling Stone *interview you mentioned that before coming back you'd*
reached the point of selling your cars.
Oh, I get it. No . . . I don't think so. You have to take into consideration the fact that I'm a very extreme person and I live in a
very extreme way. If I spend all that time hibernating, I have to
bounce back right into the other direction when I finish – go right
out in front again. It's just obvious to me knowing myself that
much. I was twitching to do something and that's the only thing I
know to do.

When I spoke to you in Harley Street towards the end of the treat-
ment, you spoke of your fears of going back on the road. You weren't
sure how you'd cope with the temptations. How did you cope?
I suppose I've been doing it for so long that it's become second
nature.

Wasn't it extra difficult?
Well, it was a little bit because we went straight into big venues. If
it had been just clubs there would have been less pressure. So, to a
certain extent, it was more difficult. Once I was in the environment
though I didn't worry about being dragged back down. I think you
can steer clear of anything if you really want to. Actually I didn't
see a lot of debauchery going on, really. The security was so tight
on the tours that you only got to meet people if you really wanted to.
Otherwise you were pretty well kept away – kept in your hotel,
straight to the gig, straight on the plane.

What's the story behind the drunkenness on-stage?
I did get smashed in New York State. I got wiped in some place. We

met up with The Band. I think it was the gig we did with The Band, and they're pretty hard drinkers. I think they drank me under the table one night.

Did the same sort of thing happen in Australia?
It happens quite a lot in most places.

Is it a reaction to coming off smack so suddenly?
Bullshit. No, I've been drinking hard since I was fifteen. It's a pretty vicious circle. Vicious? No, it's quite nice really! I went from drinking to taking pills to taking something else. There's always some kind of buzz going on. I don't think I've spent more than a week of my life when I haven't been tampering around with something. This kind of environment (Bahamas) is pretty healthy though and you don't feel you need to get out of it.

Why did you choose Dynamic Studios to record 'One In Every Crowd'?
I think it was suggested by Tom Dowd. He actually had originally wanted to go to South America, but it was impractical because there was an epidemic of spinal meningitis and so we chose to go to Kingston (Jamaica) because we thought we could pick up on reggae.

So how does the situation of a studio, the environment surrounding it, affect the recording?
Not as much as it should do, really, because once you're in there you're sealed off and you could be anywhere in the world.

But afterwards you might go out to a club and hear some local music and you'd hear a different type of music on the radio.
Yeh ... but once you're back in the studio it's just you and your music. I think you always try and preserve something of your own because you could easily get swamped by an environment. If you had wanted to you could have gone to Jamaica and done an album of complete reggae – if we didn't have anything better to do.

When did you start to pick up on reggae?
I think 'Shanty Town' was the first time I'd heard decent reggae and that was years ago. But you didn't hear much of it around for a while. You could only hear it in Birmingham or the East End where there were a lot of spades living.

How do the Jamaican natives feel about you recording reggae numbers?

The Rastas live in the hills and you don't come across them. They don't want to see anyone because they've got all their grass up there and they're in a very tricky situation because they're always armed. So the people you meet in the street, in the towns and the country, are just pretty much like people anywhere. They're nothing like the Rastas. They're city Rastas but they're pretty shallow people.

They've never accused you of ripping them off, then?

I sometimes got that feeling, but they never actually came out with it. Most of the Jamaicans we met though were pretty pleased . . . that we were promoting their music.

Was 'Swing Low Sweet Chariot' released as a single in the US?

I didn't even know it'd been put out in England until someone told me after I'd got there. I actually didn't think there was the need for a single. I still don't. I think singles are the sort of thing I like to put out once every two years and that's it. I just don't think I'm in that market. I think it's a waste of time. If they get the idea that they can put singles out from every album then we'll get three singles come off this album within three months and they'll all sell badly.

What was '461 Ocean Boulevard' originally titled?

Oh we had 'Feed The Cook' . . . 'When Pinky Get The Blues' . . . (laughs). There was another one too . . . but I can't remember it.

'One In Every Crowd' was going to be called . . .

'The Best Guitarist In The World – There's One In Every Crowd'. They didn't approve of that one either. I was the only one that thought it would be a good idea. In fact, I'm not sure whether I could have lived with it. Most people would have taken it the wrong way. They would have thought I was being serious. But I am! I am the best fucking guitarist in the world!! (Laughs.) I keep on telling myself!

Who performed the original version of 'We've Been Told That Jesus Is Coming Soon'?

Blind Willie Johnson. He was a street singer. He was a preacher and gospel singer and he used to stand outside churches to try and stop the people from going in. I don't know his real story, but he could have been a preacher that was thrown out of churches because he had rebellious ideas and then he stood outside of church all day singing.

The album you took the song from – was that a collection of Spirituals?

No, just one side. On the other side his wife was talking about him because she was still alive when they compiled the album. It's a fucking tragic story. It's another Bessie Smith number where they wouldn't let him in the hospital. He died of burns and they wouldn't take him in. He was living in a shack and it caught fire and they wouldn't take him to hospital.

Who's the Jim Byfield that wrote 'Little Rachel'?

He's a Tulsonian. He just writes songs and sells them where he can. J. J. Cale – he's another cat from Tulsa. They're both pretty relaxed. Well, there's a sort of cross-section. There's church music, soul, country and western. It's just a big melting pot. It really is right in the middle of everything. It's in Oklahoma, right smack dab in the middle of America, just about mile for mile.

Have you seen 'Tommy' since the British premiere?

Yeh. We saw it in Australia. I took the band to see it because they hadn't seen it.

And you still enjoyed it?

Fucking great. I enjoyed it even more the second time actually.

How long did it take you to film your part?

Only three days. Well, actually, he had me down for three days but I did it in two and I just hung around for the third to see what was going on – make a pest of myself. The filming bit is really strange because they call you so early in the morning just in case something might happen, but of course you're still there at ten o'clock at night waiting for them to get the spots lined up. By that time you couldn't give a damn whether you do it or not.

Was your part filmed in a deserted church?

It was a church on an army base. It was heavy. We shared the sergeants' mess. Moon and Townshend and those people were crazed. We finally frightened them out of there though. We got 'em all out.

Why were you chosen for that particular role?
I think Pete chose me.

He thought you'd make an ideal preacher?
Yeh (laughs).

Did he think that fitted you?
No, I think it was the song he thought fitted me because it's the only one he didn't write and it's written by Sonny Boy Williamson. It's a blues, you know. I think he just thought that I could do that better than anything else, and I think he wanted me to be in it as a mate because he wanted all his mates to do it. I don't think it was the role as much as the interpretation of the song, because I found it very difficult to do. It's a pretty strange song if you're going to act a preacher and sing a song like that.

I wondered whether they'd had the mystical image of you?
I doubt it. I don't think Pete's got a mystical image of me at all.

My own opinion was that 'Tommy' went too far too often.
Oh, you should have seen what it could have been like. He (Russell) gets very carried away. He has to have this guy on the set who keeps telling him to stop. A supervisor character telling him, 'No we can't do that, it's too much.'

A budget supervisor?
Not exactly. Not even that. A reality supervisor! If he'd have had his own way it wouldn't have necessarily been better but it would have been longer. And there would have been no continuity.

When do you go back on tour?
Next Saturday. Well, rehearsals begin then . . . in Miami. I had a whole list of things I wanted to rehearse and now I've forgotten them all. There's one thing I know I wanted to do and that is to wrap up all the old stuff like 'Badge' and 'Blues Power' and put

105

them in one little lump. A medley. Get them out of the way so that we can do new things.

Have you written new material since 'There's One In Every Crowd'?

Nothing really finished. Just odds and sods. I suppose we've got one song that we could go in and record tomorrow. The rest is a construction job, and I really think the worse thing in the world is to finish a song and know that as you've just put an album out, your next one is not due for another seven or eight months. I don't like things just sitting in the can because you go back and review them, and then you've got to do them all over again because you think you can do better. You might not be able to but it's just there festering, and I'd rather record things fresh and have them out as quick as possible before I can change my mind.

But the other side of the coin is that you might record a song fresh, take it out on the road for six months where you perfect it, and then wish that was on record rather than the early stages.

Yeh, that sometimes happens although very rarely.

(Enter George Terry – guitarist with the Eric Clapton Band)
George Terry: It usually works the other way. You get the spontaneity the first time around and you come up with parts that are really good and you'd never play it the same again.

Sometimes you do things that you just can't do on-stage. Things you can't really construct.

You'd obviously say that however much you performed the songs on 'Layla' you'd never better the studio album, wouldn't you?

No, of course I'd never better that. The satisfaction I got out of doing it. It would be different, that's all. That's the best you could hope for – that you could make it differently and make it good but you'd never get it better. It's a wasted exercise really. I used to think 'what would it be like if The Beatles went and cut "Love Me Do" the way they played in '67?', but I mean it would just be a different song. It wouldn't be better.

How long's this tour?

I should imagine a month. What'll happen is that it'll start out that we're booked to do three weeks and then at the end of that time we'll get options. They'll say, 'Well, how do you feel Eric? Do you feel you could play a bit more or do you really feel whacked, do you want to go home now?' Well I'll be drunk and I'll say, 'Oh, fuck, I'll do another two years.' and suddenly you've got another two years.

Did you get any further with getting into China?

We actually got a reply from the Embassy which is apparently more than a lot of people ever get. It actually was rather polite, very nice. George Patterson reckons I've got a foot in the door. If you get a reply that's courteous you've got your foot in the door. That means to say that in five years time they might be looking for someone and you might be on their list.

Did you also try South America?

I think we were going to do South America. They get into some strange things out there. All that voodoo lives there. Rio is a main city but it's pretty cosmopolitan like New York. If you get out to other parts of Brazil there's a lot of strange things going on that are pretty inexplicable. I took a picture of Nello (Pattie) as she was walking down a hill and we had it developed and there was a fucking saucer in the sky. It wasn't there when I took the picture. It's just this oval shape in the sky like a round white light on the ceiling. That floored me.

What was it that you liked about Rio that made you want to record there?

I'd never been there. I think Robert (Stigwood) made the suggestion and then Tom (Dowd) thought it was a good idea because he liked the music, but then when I got there I thought it was a pretty crummy place – Rio itself. So we spent three days there and went to a place called Bahia, which is further up the coast and has just local people – no skyscrapers and shit like that. The music was good though. While I was there they were practising for the Carnival and I recorded some of them. It's like African music. Just drums – a drum band.

Albhy: Have you told him about the Iron Men? Has that ever come up?

There's a couple of tracks on 'One In Every Crowd' where we needed percussionists around and they got these guys in called the Iron Men who play hub caps and spanners and wheel wrenches.

George: They came in with a tool box and I thought they'd come to fix the plumbing. I said 'Who are these guys?' and they said 'Oh, they're the Iron Men.' I said, 'Great, bathroom's this way' (laughs).

They're credited on the album. They played on 'Singing The Blues' and 'High'.

Were any other local musicians used?
Our security guard was pretty fucking good actually. He plays anything and everything (laughs). Peter Tosh, who is a former member of The Wailers, played on 'Don't Blame Me'.

Have you met Bob Marley?
No. I think I've met all the others though. When we were in Kingston he was in LA and when I was in New York he was in LA again. I've spoken to him on the phone. It was pretty hard to understand him on the phone. He talks a dialect. He talks his language. It's probably easier for an Englishman to understand than anyone else because there's a lot of English in it – it's just been reshaped.

Is there good music here in the Bahamas?
Bahamian music leaves a lot to be desired. It's very second-hand.

Did you choose this place for it's closeness to Miami without actually being in the US?
Yeh. So I could be with the old woman and commute if necessary.

Will you record the next album at Criteria?
It's very likely. It's become a sort of home for the band . . . unless it changes around. The trouble with places like that is that you come to rely on them to be what they are and you suddenly go back and they've changed it. Like half the studio has been changed into something else or it's suddenly not like it was. It's pretty tricky to go on recreating those sort of situations.

George Terry is a Criteria guy?
Yeh. He lives in Miami and that's where I met him. It was at the 'Layla' sessions but I don't even remember that. Albhy reminded me that he came into the studio one day with him.

108

When I was interviewing you the first time you had no idea what you were going to record and you went off with no songs and just got the band together on the spot.

Carl Radle was guaranteed to turn up with Jamie and Dickie but I got there a week ahead of them because they'd had sessions to fulfil in Tulsa. I just wanted to mess about and the band started forming before they even got there. They didn't expect that. Carl thought it was just going to be a four-piece and so we really had to sit down and deliberate it all because no one was too keen on the idea at first. It was just when we started getting going that it worked.

The relaxed sound you've got going now still reflects the culture around it, doesn't it?

How do you mean? What kind of culture?

In the mid-sixties Cream reflected the aggression and the acid involvement and then probably 'Layla' reflected the aftermath of that – the disillusionment, the failure of the 'love' thing, the involvement with harder drugs. Now there's no campus upheaval, no Kent State, no riots and there's an uneasy relaxed feel about things.

That's true, I suppose. I suppose you can't help but reflect what's going on even if you try.

Some people seem to manage to avoid it. But then you're very much a 'child of the times' getting involved with whatever's on at the time.

Yeh. I do go looking for trouble – there's no doubt about that. (Laughs.)

Living here should reflect a more relaxed feel. You're a content man!

Yeh (unsure . . . laughs). I was pretty uncomfortable here for a few days because I didn't want to leave home. That place is such a home base for me, it really is. After the first week on the road I get the homesick blues really bad every time. I just don't want to do anymore. I want to go home. That's a stage I go through every time. It takes a couple of days to wear off and then I'm all right. The first couple of days I was here I just went around criticising everything saying, 'Look at this religiosity everywhere, and the American furniture, and look at those lamps and there's no hot water and . . .

109

why isn't this,' and so on. It wasn't really that bad, it was just that I didn't want to be here.

I'd never imagined you as a home-based creature.

Well, I never was but I am now I suppose. I'm just maturing out. There comes a time.

Can you imagine being forty?

No, I can't imagine what it's like to be forty. I don't suppose it's really much different except that you just can't do as much as you could when you were thirty.

Like you can't do things now that you did when you were twenty?

I certainly can't. Things like playing badminton. I get tired very quickly. I never used to. I used to be able to do a lot more than I can do now. That's because I've lived hard – in excess all the time but it's also to do with age I should imagine.

Also at thirty most of your friends have become domesticated and things are narrowing down a lot. At twenty everyone's hanging out.

It's a stupid thing if you want to carry on with the action to go and hang out with younger people. It could be that maybe because I've been told that I can't live at home this year that I really want to be there. It might be just another reflection of the rebel.

If they let you stay at home. . . .

I'd come back here! Yeh (laughs). That is quite near the truth because I can remember sitting at home twiddling my thumbs thinking 'Oh fuck where's a gig. I've gotta have a gig because this nothing is driving me around the bend.' That's all right. Say if there was a way that I could do gigs in London, make enough money to survive and go home every night I'd probably get on with that. I don't think that I can do without home or gig. It's got to be a balance. You asked me that question about being forty – I should imagine I'll pretty much be the same.

It's going to be pretty interesting watching the rock 'n' roll people getting to forty.

Yeh. Not many of them make it do they? Elvis is the first one as far as I know.

110

Would you say you were happier now than you've ever been?

No. I think I was probably happier before I realised what happiness was. Before happiness became something that you could realise or put into words or objects . . . which must have been at a very early age. Like one.

Discography

112

1973

In Concert   Derek and The Dominos   RSO 2659 020
Eric Clapton's Rainbow Concert   RSO 2394 116

1974

461 Ocean Boulevard   Eric Clapton   RSO 2479 118

1975

There's One In Every Crowd   Eric Clapton   RSO 2479 132

Compilations and Anthologies

1966

What's Shakin'   Various Artists   Elecktra EKS 74002
Having A Rave Up With The Yardbirds   EPIC BN 26177

1967

The Yardbirds Greatest Hits   Epic BN 26246
Raw Blues   (Various Artists)   Ace of Clubs SCL 1220

1969

Best Of Cream   Polydor 583 060
World Of Blues Power Volume 3   (Various Artists)   Decca SPA 263

1970

Looking Back   John Mayall   Decca SKL 5010
The World Of John Mayall   Volume 1   Decca SPA 47

1971

The World Of John Mayall   Volume 2   Decca SPA 138
Through The Years   John Mayall   Decca SKL 5086
Remember The Yardbirds   Starline SRS 5069

1972

The History Of Eric Clapton   Polydor 2659 012
Eric Clapton At His Best   RSO 2659 025
The World Of Blues Power   Volume 3   Decca SPA 263

1973

The Best Of Delaney & Bonnie   Atlantic K 40429
Heavy Cream   Polydor 2659022

1975

The Blues World Of Eric Clapton   Decca SPA 387

Sessions

1967

Only In It For The Money   Mothers Of Invention (speaking role only)
Verve 2317 034

1968

Lady Soul   Aretha Franklin   Atlantic K40016
Bobby Whitlock   Dunhill DSX 50121
Wonderwall   George Harrison   Apple (deleted)

1969

From New Orleans to Chicago   Champion Jack Dupree   Decca (deleted)
Is This What You Want?   Jackie Lomax   Apple (deleted)
The Beatles   Apple PCS 7068
Live Peace In Toronto   Plastic Ono Band   Apple CORE 2001
Raw Velvet Bobby Whitlock   Dunhill DSX 50131
That's The Way God Planned It   Billy Preston   Apple (deleted)

1970

All Things Must Pass   George Harrison   Apple STCH 639/3
Get Ready   King Curtis
Stephen Stills   Atlantic 2401 004
Ain't That Cute   Doris Troy   Apple SAPCOR 13
Leon Russell   A & M AMLS 982

114

1971

Fly   Yoko Ono   Apple (deleted)
The Son Moon And Herbs   Dr John   Atlantic K40250
The Concert For Bangla Desh   Apple (deleted)
Stephen Stills 2   Atlantic 2401013
Back To The Roots   John Mayall   Polydor 2657 005

1972

Anthology   Duane Allman   Capricorn 2659 035
Some Time In New York City   John and Yoko   Apple SVBB 3392
Buddy Guy And Junior Wells Play The Blues   Atlantic K40240

1973

The London Howlin' Wolf Sessions   Howlin' Wolf   Chess (deleted)
The Last Five Years   Rick Grech   RSO 2394111

1974

Burglar   Freddie King   RSO 2394140

Singles

1964

I Wish You Would / A Certain Girl   The Yardbirds   Columbia
Good Morning Little Schoolgirl / I Ain't Got You   The Yardbirds   Columbia

1965

For Your Love / Got To Hurry   The Yardbirds   Columbia

1966

Telephone Blues / I'm Your Witchdoctor   The Bluesbreakers   Columbia
Lonely Years / Bernard Jenkins   John Mayall with Eric Clapton   Purdah
Wrapping Paper / Cat's Squirrel   Cream   Reaction
I Feel Free / NSU   Cream   Reaction

115

1967

Strange Brew / Tales Of Brave Ulysses   Cream   Reaction

1968

Anyone For Tennis / Pressed Rat And Warthog   Cream   Polydor
Sunshine Of Your Love / Swablr   Cream   Polydor

1969

White Room / Those Were The Days   Cream   Polydor
Badge / What A Bringdown   Cream   Polydor

1972

Layla / Bell Bottom Blues   Derek and The Dominos   Polydor

1974

I Shot The Sheriff / Give Me Strength   Eric Clapton   RSO
Willie And The Hand Jive / Mainline Florida   Eric Clapton   RSO
Smile   Eric Clapton   RSO   ('Prime Cuts' – a maxi-single sampler)

1975

Swing Low Sweet Chariot / Pretty Blue Eyes   Eric Clapton   RSO
Knockin' On Heaven's Door / Someone Like You   Eric Clapton   RSO

BOB DYLAN

ANTHONY SCADUTO

'This is a big, superbly detailed and important biography of the man who was one of the most powerful seminal influences on the turbulent 1960's – a brilliantly gifted Minnesota kid who came forth with a secret bag of torments to write and sing those songs whose sounds and ideas are today's household words: "Blowin' in the Wind" and "The Times They are A' Changin'" '
Publishers Weekly

75p *Illustrated*

OUT OF HIS HEAD

The Sound of Phil Spector

RICHARD WILLIAMS

'I have always admired this genius – whose talent influenced the whole music business. After reading this book I was amazed at the amount of great records he'd been involved with that had influenced me back in Liverpool . . . He is and always will be one of the great originals of rock music – and it's true – to know him *is* to love him'
John Lennon

65p *Illustrated*

ELVIS

JERRY HOPKINS

'Just about as comprehensive a book as anyone is ever likely to offer on a pop idol. This is exactly the book which legions of Presley fans will clamour for . . . The author, Jerry Hopkins, has done a tremendous job of research and collation, and has written the biography in engrossing style'
Evening News

£1·00 *Illustrated*

BESSIE
Empress of the Blues
CHRIS ALBERTSON

'The product of painstaking research, this biography of Bessie Smith
is the most devastating, provocative and enlightening work of its
kind ever contributed to the annals of jazz literature'
Los Angeles Times

£1·00   *Illustrated*

LADY SINGS THE BLUES
BILLIE HOLIDAY with WILLIAM DUFTY

'*Lady Sings The Blues* is a stark, jarring story of a Negro singer
whose impoverished background was such that she was working
before she was ten and whose turbulent life, with its narcotics, booze
and succession of men, was so lacerating that it almost exceeded
belief'
The Financial Times

£1·00   *Illustrated*

SCOTT JOPLIN AND THE RAGTIME ERA
PETER GAMMOND

'Readable, ripe with understanding and commonsense ... This is a
fine example of what a book on popular music should be: evoca-
tively designed, entertaining, informative, open-minded, careful to
demonstrate the relationships between modern musical styles'
The Sunday Times

£1·25   *Illustrated*

THE PARADE'S GONE BY . . .

KEVIN BROWNLOW

'Absorbing study of Hollywood before the talkies . . . Its illustrations are lavish and fascinating and the narrative peppered with the kind of detail that pin-points the personalities more accurately than a descriptive chapter . . . He has written a spectacular book'
Sunday Telegraph

£1·75   *Illustrated*

STANLEY KUBRICK DIRECTS

ALEXANDER WALKER

Richly illustrated with over 350 stills, which add force to the detailed analyses of style and content, this book traces the flow of Kubrick's work from *Paths of Glory* to *Dr Strangelove, 2001: A Space Odyssey* and *A Clockwork Orange*.

£1·00   *Illustrated*

THERE MUST BE A LONE RANGER

The Myth and Reality of the American Wild West

JENNI CALDER

'Most original . . . she draws not only on films but on the novels of the West from Owen Wister and Zane Grey to the present crop of Western writers, to demonstrate where the myth diverges from the reality'
The Daily Telegraph

95p   *Illustrated*

PSI: PSYCHIC DISCOVERIES BEHIND THE IRON CURTAIN

SHEILA OSTRANDER & LYNN SCHROEDER

'The most important book about ESP research and the validity of the occult tradition yet to appear'
Los Angeles Times

'This book was born to cause controversy ... Fact, fancies and fantasies are all there, woven in a vivid style that will stimulate and intrigue every imagination ... A potential bombshell'
Psychic Magazine

£1·50   *Illustrated*

THE SECRET POWERS OF PLANTS

BRETT L. BOLTON

Complete with plant cures and a special chapter on plants and astrology, *The Secret Powers of Plants* presents challenging, thought-provoking evidence of the psychic faculties of plants – secret powers that man is only just beginning to penetrate.

£1·00   *Illustrated*

THE LIFE BEYOND DEATH

ARTHUR FORD

'*The Life Beyond Death* will hold one's interest from start to finish. It is a fascinating and thought-provoking book which will be discussed long after the final chapter has been reached'
Cork Examiner

75p

THE OLD STRAIGHT TRACK

ALFRED WATKINS

The most important source book for the study of the ancient straight tracks or leys that criss-cross the British Isles – a fascinating system which was old when the Romans came to Britain.

£1·25   *Illustrated*

THE SPHINX AND THE MEGALITHS

JOHN IVIMY

'It is a detective story which takes us through the Middle East, Egypt, discussing the pre-Christian religions and their teachings, and giving an answer to the famous riddle of the Sphinx ... Mr Ivimy sifts through the evidence carefully ... creating a truly intriguing work which will fascinate all those interested in Stonehenge, and much else'
Psychic Researcher

£1·20   *Illustrated*

THE VIEW OVER ATLANTIS

JOHN MICHELL

A fascinating account of the advanced universal civilisation of pre-history, whose relics still survive throughout the world – the dragon paths of China, Irish fairy paths, straight tracks in Europe and beyond, and the 'ley' system of aligned monuments which include Stonehenge and the Great Pyramid.

£1·10   *Illustrated*

SMALL IS BEAUTIFUL

A Study of Economics as if People Mattered

E. F. SCHUMACHER

'A book of heart and hope and downright commonsense about the future . . . The basic message in this tremendously thought-provoking book is that man is pulling the earth and himself out of equilibrium by applying only one test to everything he does: money, profits, and therefore giant operations. We have got to ask instead, what about the cost in human terms, in happiness, health, beauty and conserving the planet?'
Daily Mail

£1·25

OPEN MARRIAGE

NENA O'NEILL & GEORGE O'NEILL

'*Open Marriage – A New Life Style for Couples* plants a sizeable time-bomb under traditional concepts, without denying the necessity of marriage itself . . . I guarantee that every marriage has something to learn from the O'Neills'
Daily Express

90p

ONE DIMENSIONAL MAN

HERBERT MARCUSE

'A "classic" of social criticism . . . The analysis he presents is impressive without doubt . . . for the ferocity and power with which he reveals the pervasive alienation and un-freedom of modern technological society'
Peace News

75p

GYPSIES

JEREMY SANDFORD

'This collection of documents brings vividly before us the astonishing vigour of Romany culture, its pride and colour, its wit and tenacity, and, alongside that, the "squalor of rubbish tips and refuse dumps . . . the endless series of evictions . . . the sprawl and concrete of our local authority sites", which now forms its real environment'
New Society

£1·10   *Illustrated*

THE TRIBE THAT HIDES FROM MAN

ADRIAN COWELL

'It is so superbly written, and so warm with affection and bright with intelligence, that it conveys more movingly and precisely than any camera could do the tragic inevitability of the Indians' extinction . . . Mr Cowell's book is both a penetrating study of anthropological dilemmas and an intensely exciting adventure story'
The Irish Times

£1·40   *Illustrated*

YASIR ARAFAT

THOMAS KIERNAN

The first biography of the leader of the Palestinian Liberation Organisation – the man hailed as the hero of the Palestinian cause and as representative of terrorism and violence. Describing the history and evolution of the P.L.O., Thomas Kiernan tells the inside story of the *real* organisation and provides insight into its true position in the Middle East.

95p

THE PRIMAL SCREAM

ARTHUR JANOV

'Several times a century a book appears which holds promise of reshaping society . . . One such book has just been released which in the field of psychology could wield as much influence as the early writings of Sigmund Freud and probably work to a much better end'
Berkeley Gazette

95p

THE BOOK ON THE TABOO AGAINST KNOWING WHO YOU ARE

ALAN WATTS

'This lovely and humorous work will shock, outrage, excite, delight and profoundly stimulate anyone who has ever asked "Who or What am I?"'
The Irish Press

65p

GOLF IN THE KINGDOM

MICHAEL MURPHY

'This is the Western equivalent of Herrigel's famous *Zen in the Art of Archery*, but a much better book, in which a sport is employed as a yoga or spiritual discipline. Furthermore, the writing is so fine that one can smell the heather and the whisky and feel the intense human warmth of all the characters involved'
Alan Watts

95p

BIOFEEDBACK
Turning On the Power of your Mind
MARVIN KARLINS & LEWIS M. ANDREWS

Biofeedback discusses in depth a revolutionary new technique which allows you to change and control the state of your health, happiness and well-being solely through the power of your mind, without the use of medicine or drugs.

75p

AS MAN BECOMES MACHINE
DAVID RORVIK

Surveying the state of current research – including ESB (electronic stimulation of the brain), BFT (biofeedback training), telefactors and total prosthesis – David Rorvik explores the frightening implications of a future world where Man and Machine will cease to exist as separate entities and will become one, a world where experimental science and science fiction merge.

£1·00

TOTAL MAN
STAN GOOCH

'Drawing on literature and legend, on science fiction, mythology, history, physiology, linguistics and art, British psychologist Stan Gooch has written a daring new interpretation of the human psyche ... His book presents a rare attempt at providing a complete system of thought aimed at fostering the evolution of a "new consciousness"'
Publishers Weekly

£1·60

To
Jack,
Merry Christmas!
Love,

· ·

'Twas the night before Christmas,
when all through the house,
Not a creature was stirring,
not even a mouse;
Jack's stocking was hung
by the chimney with care,
In hope that St. Nicholas
soon would be there.

Jack was nestled all snug in his bed,
While visions of candy canes danced in his head.
And Mom in her kerchief, and Dad in his cap,
Had just settled down for a long winter's nap.

When out on the street
there arose such a clatter,
Jack sprang from his bed
to see what was the matter.
Away to the window
Jack flew like a flash,
Tore open the curtains,
threw open the latch.

The moon on the blanket
of new-fallen snow,
Shone bright as midday
on the objects below—

When, what to Jack's
wondering eyes should appear,
But a miniature sleigh
and eight tiny reindeer.

With a little old driver,
so lively and quick,
Jack knew in a moment
it must be St. Nick.
More rapid than eagles
his reindeer they came,
And he whistled, and shouted,
and called them by name:

To
Jack

"Now, Dasher! Now, Dancer!
Now, Prancer and Vixen!
On, Comet! On, Cupid!
On, Donder and Blitzen!
Take me up to Jack's chimney; follow my call!
Now dash away, dash away, dash away all!"

And then, in a twinkling,
Jack heard on the roof
The prancing and pawing
of each little hoof.

As Jack pulled in his head
and was turning around,
Down the chimney
St. Nicholas came with a bound.

He was dressed all in fur,
from his head to his foot,
And his clothes were all tarnished
with ashes and soot.
A bundle of toys he had
flung on his back,
And he looked like a peddler
holding his pack.

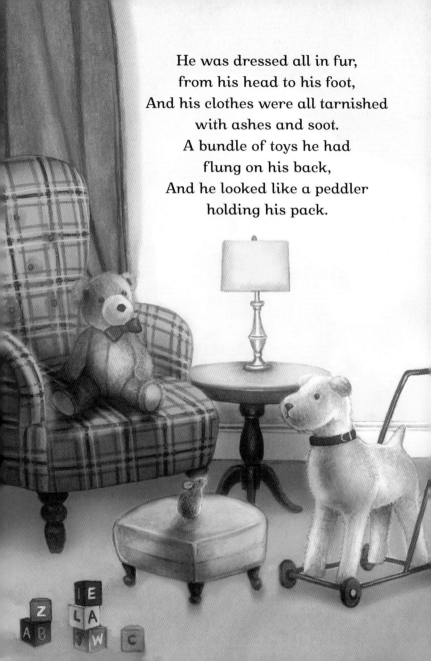

To
Jack

His eyes—how they twinkled!
His dimples—how merry!
His cheeks were like roses,
his nose like a cherry.
His droll little mouth
was drawn up like a bow,
And the beard on his chin was
as white as the snow.

Dear Santa,
I hope you enjoy
the sweet treats.
Love,
Jack

P.S. The carrots
are for your
furry friends.

A big sack of toys
he held tight in his fist,
And he glanced to see Jack
at the top of his list.
He had a broad face
and a little round belly
That shook when he laughed,
like a bowl full of jelly.

Jack

NICE LIST
Jack
Steven
Glenn
Marcus
Lorenzo

He was chubby and plump,
a right jolly old elf,
And Jack laughed when he saw him,
in spite of himself.

St. Nick winked an eye
and tilted his head
Letting Jack know
he had nothing to dread.

He spoke not a word,
but went straight to his work,
And filled up Jack's stocking,
then turned with a jerk.

Jack

And tapping his finger at the side of his nose,
And giving a nod, up the chimney he rose.

He sprang to his sleigh, to his team gave a whistle,
And away they all flew like the down of a thistle.
But St. Nicholas exclaimed, as he drove out of sight—

"Merry Christmas to Jack,
and to all a good night!"

Jack, draw all your favorite
Christmas presents from Santa.

Adapted from the poem by Clement C. Moore
Illustrated by Lisa Alderson
Designed by Jane Gollner

Copyright © Hometown World Ltd. 2019

Put Me In The Story is a
registered trademark of Sourcebooks, Inc.
All rights reserved.

Published by Put Me In The Story,
a publication of Sourcebooks, Inc.
P.O. Box 4410, Naperville, Illinois 60567-4410
(630) 536-1104
www.putmeinthestory.com

Date of Production: July 2019
Run Number: 5015191
Printed and bound in Italy (LG)
10 9 8 7 6 5 4 3 2 1

MIX
Paper from
responsible sources
FSC® C023419
www.fsc.org

Bestselling books starring your child!
www.putmeinthestory.com